Copy Editor & Interior Design: Constance Santego
Book Layout: ©2017 BookDesignTemplates.com

Ordering Information:
Quantity sales. Special discounts are available on quantity purchases by corporations, associations, and others. For details, contact the "Special Sales Department" at the address above.

Trade Paperback ISBN: 978-1-997907-08-4
Ebook ISBN 978-1-997907-09-1
Created and published In Canada. Printed and bound in the United States of America

First Edition
Published by Maximillian Enterprises
Kelowna, BC
Canada
www.constancesantego.ca

CONFIDENCE – MASTERING THE DREAM METHOD

*Not just manifesting dreams—
living them with confidence.*

Vol II

Dr. Constance Santego

Maximillian Enterprises
Kelowna, BC

Dedication

To everyone learning to trust themselves again—
May you remember that confidence is not something you find,
but something you choose, moment by moment,
until it becomes who you are.

— Dr. Constance Santego

ALSO BY DR. CONSTANCE SANTEGO

NOVELS
Illegitimate Grace
Ashcroft Hollow

Okanagan Trilogy:
Beneath the Vineyards
Under the Okanagan Sun
Guardian of the Lake

The Nine Spiritual Gifts Series:
Journey of a Soul – (Vol 1 Michael)
Language of a Soul – (Vol 2 Gabriel)
Prophecy of a Soul – (Vol 3 Bath Kol)
Healing of a Soul – (Vol 4 Raphael)
Miracles of a Soul – (Vol 5 Hamied)
Knowledge of a Soul – (Vol 6 Raziel)
Wisdom of a Soul – (Vol 7 Uriel)
Faith of a Soul – (Vol 8 Pistis Sophia)

NONFICTION
The Intuitive Life, The Gift Of Prophecy, Third Edition
Fairy Tales, Dreams And Reality… Where Are You On Your Path? Second Edition
Your Persona… The Mask You Wear
Archangel Michael's Soul Retrieval Guide
Tesla And The Future Of Energy Medicine
Beyond Tesla: Advancing The Science Of Energy Healing
Tesla's Code: Mastering Energy, Frequency, And Creative Power
Beyond The Mind: Harnessing The Power Of Astral Projection For Creative Awakening
Bend, Don't Break: Finding Your Way Back To Abundance
Ring Therapy: A Guide To Healing And Balance
Ring Therapy Pocket Guide
Floraopathy™: The Art And Science Of Vibrational Healing With Essential Oils
Dear Older Me: A Memoir… Of Sorts
It's Just Like Poker: A Spiritual Guide To Playing The Cards Life Deals You
Signs And Meanings: What The Feet Reveal About Health, Stress, And The Body's Story
Auricions: Unlocking Subconscious Healing Through Quantum Medicine
Quick Fix Acupressure Method
Manifestation – The DREAM Method in 5 Steps
The New Paradigm: Conscious Healing In The Age Of AI

REIKI WISDOM, SERIES:
Angelic Lifestyle, a Vibrant Lifestyle
Angelic Lifestyle 42-Day Energy Cleanse
Reiki and the Power of The Joint Points: Unlocking Energy Pathways for
Healing (Vol I)
Reiki and Karmic Healing: Releasing Patterns From Past Lives (Vol II)
Reiki and the Five Elements (Vol III)
Secrets of a Healer, Magic Of Reiki
The Reiki Master's Manual

CHAKRA SERIES:
Heart Chakra 101: The Bridge
Root Chakra 101: Building Safety, Survival, Foundation
Sacral Chakra 101: Creativity, Pleasure, Emotions
Solar Plexus Chakra 101: Power, Confidence, Will
Throat Chakra 101: Truth, Voice, Self-Expression
Third Eye Chakra 10: Intuition, Vision, Insight
Crown Chakra 10: Spiritual Connection, Transcendence.

SECRETS OF A HEALER, SERIES:
Magic Of Aromatherapy (Vol I)
Magic Of Reflexology (Vol II)
Magic Of The Gifts (Vol III)
Magic Of Muscle Testing (Vol IV)
Magic Of Iridology (Vol V)
Magic Of Massage (Vol VI)
Magic Of Hypnotherapy (Vol VII)
Magic Of Reiki (Vol VIII)
Magic Of Advanced Aromatherapy (Vol IX)
Magic Of Esthetics (Vol X)
The Reiki Master's Manual (Vol XI)

ADULT COLORING JOURNALS
SERIES-ZEN COLORING:
Quantum Energy and Mindful Living Journal (Vol 1)
Reiki Energy Journal (Vol 2)
Nine Spiritual Gifts Journal (Vol 3)
I Forgive Journal (Vol 4)

FOR CHILDREN
I am Big Tonight. I Don't Need the Light
The Magic Elf Book: 25 Days of Surprises

COOKBOOK
My Favorite Recipes, with a Hint of Giggle

BUISNESS
How To Use ChatGPT For Authors: From Idea To Published Book
Scaling Beyond 6 Figures: Strategies For Health & Wellness Professionals
The Academypreneur's Playbook: Turn Knowledge Into A
Revenue-Generating School

HUMOR/GIFT BOOK
How Do You Like Your Eggs? *Crack Into Your Personality, Yolk and All*

Contents

Preface

When I first introduced *Manifestation – The DREAM Method in 5 Steps*, I created a roadmap to help people move from dreaming to doing, from wishing to creating. The DREAM Method—Define, Release, Envision, Align, and Master—was designed to guide anyone through the manifestation process with clarity and confidence.

But as I taught and worked with readers, one truth became clear: **the fifth step, Mastery, is the most misunderstood and the most transformative.** Too often, people believe manifestation ends when they "get" what they asked for. The new job, the partner, the opportunity, the breakthrough—it arrives, and they assume the process is complete. But manifestation isn't complete until the lesson of the experience is integrated.

Step Five is where you pause, reflect, refine, and repeat. It is where you ask:

- *What did this manifestation teach me?*
- *How have I changed as a result of it?*
- *Is this truly what I wanted—or simply what I thought I wanted?*

When Step Five is skipped, success can feel hollow, or worse, it can inflate the ego. The energy of manifestation, left unreflected, can tip into arrogance, entitlement, or even the drug of power—narcissism. When Step Five is embraced, however, manifestation matures into confidence: grounded, generous, and lasting.

This book is my response to that realization. Here, I go deeper into Step Five. I will show you how to recognize when reflection turns negative, how to clear the emotions, patterns, and energies that block your manifestations, and how to step fully into your authentic power without losing your humility.

You do not need to have read my first book to understand or benefit from this one. Think of that book as the map, and this one as the compass. Together, they guide you not only toward your dreams, but toward mastery of yourself—where confidence, clarity, and empowerment can thrive without tipping into ego.

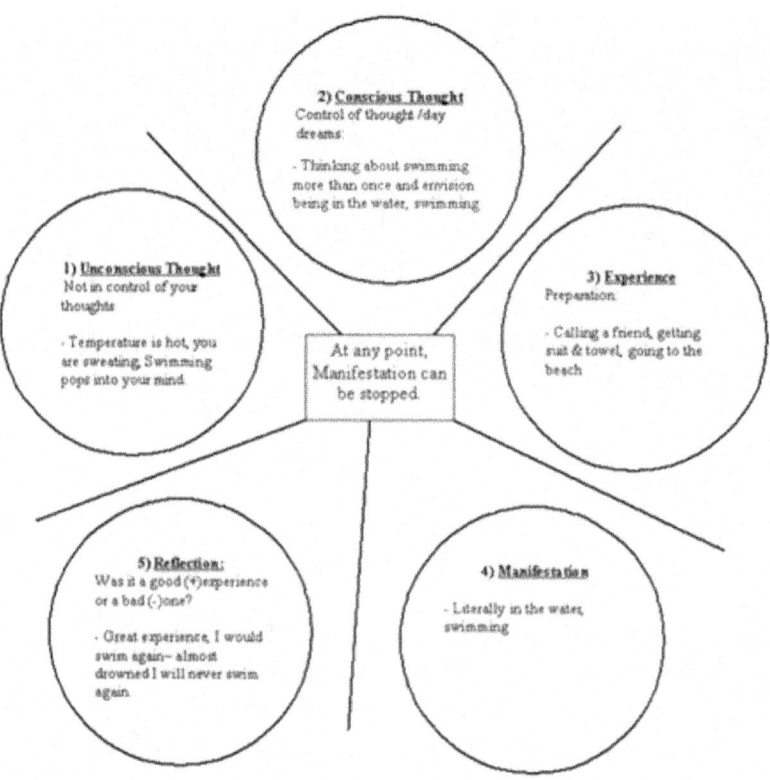

Note to Reader

This book is not here to tell you who you should be—it is here to remind you of who you already are.

As you move through these pages, you may notice old patterns rising: doubt, resistance, even defensiveness. That's normal. These are not signs that you are failing; they are signs that you are meeting the very blocks this book is meant to help you clear.

Take your time. Some sections may resonate immediately, others may ask you to pause and reflect. Go gently, but also go honestly. The practices shared here are not meant to be done all at once. They are tools you can return to again and again, each time meeting yourself at a deeper level of truth.

Remember:

- You don't need to be perfect to be powerful.
- You don't need to know everything to begin.
- You don't need to fear your ego—you only need to learn how to guide it.

Keep this book close, not as a set of rules, but as a companion on your journey. Let it serve as a mirror, reflecting your strength, your humility, and the unique way only you can embody true power.

With warmth and belief in your becoming,
Dr. Constance Santego

How to Use This Book

This is not a book to race through—it's a book to work with. Each chapter is designed to help you reflect, release, and realign so you can hold your power without slipping into arrogance, entitlement, or ego-driven patterns.

Here's how to get the most from these pages:

1. Read Actively

Keep a journal nearby. As you read, capture insights, emotions, or blocks that rise to the surface. The act of writing anchors awareness and speeds integration.

2. Practice the Exercises

Throughout the book, you'll find practical tools—emotional, mental, and energetic clearing methods. Don't just read them—*do them.* Even a few minutes of practice can create a noticeable shift.

3. Go at Your Own Pace

Some chapters may feel light; others may stir deeper emotions or resistance. Move at a pace that honors your nervous system. Return to sections whenever you need reinforcement.

4. Use as a Reference

This book is both a journey and a toolkit. After your first read, come back and use specific practices whenever you notice a block—whether it's disappointment, jealousy, perfectionism, or energetic heaviness.

5. Stay Curious, Not Critical

You may discover patterns you didn't realize were shaping your manifestations. Approach them with curiosity, not judgment. Every block you uncover is an invitation to deeper freedom.

Important Reminder:
You don't need to clear every block perfectly to manifest. Progress, not perfection, is what keeps energy flowing. Each time you reflect and release, you strengthen your ability to stay in your power with humility, clarity, and grace.

CONFIDENCE – MASTERING THE DREAM METHOD

*Not just manifesting dreams—
living them with confidence.*

Vol II

Dr. Constance Santego

Introduction

Have you ever achieved something you thought would change everything— a relationship, a job, a financial breakthrough— only to feel the excitement fade too quickly?

Instead of fulfillment, you felt emptiness. Instead of gratitude, you slipped into comparison or self-criticism. Instead of confidence, you caught yourself clinging to control, demanding more, or fearing it would all disappear.

You're not alone. Many seekers on the path of manifestation and empowerment run into this very wall. Success arrives, but without reflection, it doesn't last. The high of achievement turns into disappointment. Desire turns into demand. And what was meant to expand you instead begins to harden you.

This is the hidden trap of empowerment: without integration, power bends toward ego. It shows up as entitlement, arrogance, or even narcissism—the drug of false power. You get what you want, but it doesn't feel like enough. You shine brightly, but only for a moment, before shadows creep back in.

But it doesn't have to be this way.

True empowerment doesn't strip you of humility—it deepens it. It doesn't leave you chasing the next win—it allows you to hold and savor what you've created. It doesn't demand control—it flows with life, aligning your inner authority with the greater rhythm of the universe.

This book is your invitation into that alignment. Here, you'll learn how to recognize the subtle ways ego hijacks your power—and more importantly, how to clear the emotional, mental, and energetic blocks that sabotage your manifestations. You'll discover practices to release resentment, jealousy, self-doubt, and heaviness so that what you manifest not only comes to you, but stays with you.

Because empowerment is not about getting louder, richer, or stronger. Empowerment is about becoming rooted, aligned, and free.

A TALE OF TWO ENTREPRENEURS

Imagine two women, both starting their dream businesses.

The first woman builds from external control. She micromanages every employee, checks emails obsessively, and believes nothing will work unless she forces it. At first, she sees results—the business opens quickly, money flows in—but behind the scenes, her staff feels drained, and her own exhaustion grows. Within a year, her manifestation begins to slip. What looked strong on the surface was built on fear and force.

The second woman builds from inner authority. She takes bold, aligned action, but she also trusts her instincts and the people she hires. She knows who she is and what she stands for, so she doesn't chase every trend or second-guess every decision. She acts decisively, but not desperately. Challenges arise, but she adapts without losing her center. Her business grows steadily, not because she forced it, but because it was rooted in clarity and trust.

One manifestation collapses. The other lasts. The difference isn't luck or timing—it's foundation.

Key Insight:
Lasting manifestations are never rooted in fear. They are held by inner authority—the quiet confidence that says, *"I am aligned. I trust the process. I can sustain what I create."*

Part I – Why Manifestations Don't Last

The Foundation of Lasting Manifestation

Manifestation isn't just about calling something in—it's about being able to hold it once it arrives. Too many people achieve what they set their sights on—falling in love, buying the dream house, starting the business—only to watch it crumble. The relationship dissolves. The house becomes a financial burden. The business never stabilizes.

These losses can feel like failure, but the truth is different: the manifestation wasn't false; it simply wasn't rooted. You didn't lose it because it wasn't real—you lost it because the foundation wasn't clear.

At the root of this problem is a misunderstanding of power. Many people confuse **alignment** with **domination**, or mistake **inner authority** for **external control.** Others unconsciously buy into cultural myths—that louder means stronger, that more means better, that control equals safety. Each of these distortions creates cracks in the foundation. And when the foundation is unstable, even the most powerful manifestation can slip away.

A manifestation is only as stable as the energy that created it. If your thoughts say yes, but your emotions are still carrying old wounds, the energy is split. If your actions move forward but your beliefs whisper doubt, the current is fractured. If your heart longs for connection but your body carries fear of loss, the signal is distorted.

Think of it like building a home. You can design the most beautiful structure, but if it's built on weak ground, the walls will shift and eventually collapse. Manifestation works the same way: your desire may be clear, but without a stable energetic and emotional foundation, it cannot hold.

When your energy, beliefs, actions, and emotions move in harmony, manifestation becomes magnetic and sustainable. Life flows toward you and stays with you, because there is no resistance inside you pushing it away. But when they're fragmented, the river of manifestation floods, dries up, or slips through your fingers—leaving you wondering what went wrong.

This book exists to answer that question. It is not about whether you *can* manifest—you already can. It's about helping you build the foundation to **keep** what you create.

ALIGNMENT VS. DOMINATION

Manifestations don't slip away because they weren't real—they slip because they were built on the shaky ground of domination instead of the solid foundation of alignment.

Domination looks powerful in the moment. You push, demand, and control until something gives way. You might even get results this way—a business deal, a relationship, a win—but those results rarely last. Domination drains you because it requires constant force. Like holding a door shut against the wind, the effort never ends. Eventually, exhaustion sets in, and what you've created begins to unravel.

Alignment, on the other hand, is sustainable power. When your energy, beliefs, actions, and emotions all move in the same direction, manifestation flows naturally. You don't need to push; you allow. You don't need to control; you choose. Alignment creates a current strong enough to carry your manifestation forward long after the initial spark.

Signs of Domination (Fragile Foundation)

- Forcing outcomes instead of letting them unfold
- Needing to control how others respond

- Believing power comes from being "on top"
- Feeling drained or burnt out by constant pressure

Signs of Alignment (Lasting Foundation)

- Energy feels steady, even during challenges
- Acting with clarity rather than control
- Experiencing synchronicities and unexpected support
- Confidence feels natural, not forced

Domination can get you quick wins—but alignment is what makes them last.

INNER AUTHORITY VS. EXTERNAL CONTROL

One of the greatest reasons manifestations collapse is because people mistake **external control** for empowerment. On the surface, both can look similar: decisive action, bold choices, strong words. But their energy—and their results—are very different.

Inner authority is the power that comes from within. It is self-mastery: the quiet, steady knowing of who you are and what you stand for. It doesn't need applause, proof, or permission. It doesn't rise and fall with circumstances. Instead, it flows from alignment. When you act from inner authority, your choices feel clean, your energy feels grounded, and others often feel uplifted in your presence. Manifestations rooted in inner authority last because they are supported by truth. They rest on a foundation of trust in yourself and in life.

External control, however, is built on force. It is the attempt to bend people, circumstances, or even the universe to your will. It may work in the short term—you can demand results, push through obstacles, or pressure people into compliance—but it creates brittleness. Control breeds resistance, and resistance eventually cracks the structure you've built.

Manifestations created from external control rarely last because they are powered by fear:

- Fear of losing what you just gained.
- Fear of uncertainty or change.
- Fear that without control, you are not enough.

This fear-based energy weakens the foundation. The house may look beautiful, but its walls are hollow. The relationship may sparkle in the beginning, but hidden insecurity gnaws at it. The business may launch with a bang, but without trust and alignment, it struggles to sustain.

When you build from **inner authority**, you don't need to clutch or force. You hold your vision with clarity and trust that life is working with you, not against you. The energy feels expansive, magnetic, and liberating—not just for you, but for those around you. Others feel invited into your power, not oppressed by it.

When you build from **external control**, the manifestation feels heavy, brittle, and unstable. It requires constant vigilance, endless proving, and more and more force to keep it together. And sooner or later, the strain causes it to slip away.

Key Insight:
Lasting manifestations are never rooted in fear. They are held by inner authority—the quiet confidence that says, *"I am aligned. I trust the process. I can sustain what I create."*

Part II – Blocks

Manifestation That Lasts

Manifestation is not only about creating desires—it's about sustaining them. Many people achieve what they set out for—love, money, health, opportunity—only to watch it slip away, feel hollow, or spark a cycle they can't seem to repeat. Others wonder why the manifestation never arrived at all.

This book is for those moments—the times when you feel stuck, disappointed, or questioning whether manifestation "works" for you. The truth is, manifestation always works—but when the results don't last, it's not a failure of the process. It's a signal that something in your foundation is out of alignment.

That misalignment becomes most visible in Step Five of the DREAM Method: **Master (reflect, refine, repeat).** *Did you like the experience or not (positive + or negative - experience)?*

POSITIVE VS. NEGATIVE EXPERIENCES

Every manifestation, whether large or small, creates an *experience.* When you reflect (step 5: Master), the first question is simple: *Did I like the experience or not?*

- If it was **positive (+)**, you usually don't need to change much. Positive experiences naturally reinforce themselves. You feel gratitude, alignment deepens, and the energy of the manifestation stabilizes.
- If it was **negative (–),** that's where the challenge lies. Most people don't know how to shift a negative experience. Instead, they replay it, resist it, or bury it. This creates a **block.**

Unresolved negative experiences lodge in your system as emotional charge, limiting beliefs, energetic imbalance, or even physical tension. They don't just vanish over time—they wait until the next cycle of manifestation and resurface, quietly sabotaging the foundation.

Lasting manifestation doesn't mean you never have negative experiences. It means you learn how to clear and transform them so they no longer block the flow. Positive experiences stabilize what you've created. Negative experiences, when processed, strengthen your foundation and prevent it from collapsing.

PRINCIPLE: YOU DON'T CLEAR THE DESIRE— YOU CLEAR THE BLOCK

When manifestation doesn't seem to work—or when it arrives but slips away—many people assume the problem is the desire itself. They tell themselves:

- *"Maybe it wasn't meant for me."*
- *"Maybe I asked for too much."*
- *"Maybe I need to settle for less."*

But this isn't true. **Desire itself is not the problem.** Desire is a compass pointing toward your soul's growth. It shows you the next layer of expansion waiting to unfold.

What blocks manifestation isn't the dream—it's the resistance sitting on top of it. And unless that resistance is cleared, even if the desire arrives, it won't last.

The work of Step Five isn't about shrinking your vision or lowering your expectations. It's about identifying and releasing the hidden weight that prevents you from holding what you've created.

- If disappointment blocks gratitude, you clear the disappointment.

- If resentment poisons fulfillment, you clear the resentment.
- If scarcity beliefs sabotage abundance, you clear the scarcity pattern.
- If the demand for energy creates an imbalance, you restore alignment.
- If others' manifestations conflict with yours, you disentangle and reset your field.

The desire remains intact. The dream is still valid. Once the block is removed, manifestation doesn't just return—it becomes sustainable. It has room to breathe, grow, and stay.

SUCCESS STORIES THAT LAST

Entertainment & Media
Oprah Winfrey – From Poverty to Media Mogul

Oprah was born into poverty in rural Mississippi, raised by a single mother, and faced layers of trauma and hardship. She began with nothing—not even stability at home. Yet, through her vision, relentless belief in her purpose, and her ability to connect authentically, she didn't just manifest a career in television—she built a global media empire. Her dream of "sharing stories that matter" went far beyond hosting a talk show; it became a worldwide legacy of empowerment, philanthropy, and influence.

Tyler Perry – Homeless to Hollywood

Tyler Perry once lived in his car while struggling to get his plays noticed. He poured his life savings into productions that failed repeatedly. Still, he believed in his vision. That persistence birthed the Madea character and eventually his own film studio—the first fully Black-owned major film studio in the U.S. His dream grew beyond acting or writing: it became about ownership, legacy, and lifting others.

In Business & Innovation

Howard Schultz – Coffee Shop to Global Brand

Howard Schultz grew up in public housing in Brooklyn. When he discovered a small coffee shop in Seattle called Starbucks, he had a vision of bringing European-style coffee culture to America. At first, investors doubted him. Yet, his clarity and persistence transformed a single store into a global brand with over 30,000 locations. His dream wasn't just to sell coffee—it was to create a community experience.

- **Sara Blakely (Spanx Founder):** Started with $5,000 in savings, selling fax machines door-to-door. She believed in her idea for women's shapewear when no one else did. Today, Spanx is a billion-dollar brand, and she became the world's youngest female self-made billionaire at the time.
- **Elon Musk:** Despite early failures (like nearly bankrupting Tesla in 2008), he held to his vision of electric cars and space exploration. Now Tesla, SpaceX, and SolarCity have reshaped multiple industries.
- **Steve Jobs:** Dropped out of college, started Apple in a garage. Even after being fired from his own company, he returned and transformed Apple into one of the most valuable brands on the planet.

In Music & Entertainment

Lady Gaga – Rejected Before Fame

Before becoming an icon, Lady Gaga (Stefani Germanotta) was dropped from her first record label after only a few months. She performed in clubs, often dismissed for being "too weird." But her vision and certainty in her artistry didn't fade. She manifested not only a music career but an entire cultural movement—fusing music, fashion, performance, and activism—creating a platform far larger than just singing.

- **Ed Sheeran:** Slept on friends' couches while performing small gigs. He manifested not just a music career but a global following, stadium tours, and multiple Grammy awards.
- **Rihanna:** Came from a small island (Barbados) with no industry connections. She not only became a global superstar but also expanded into fashion and beauty (Fenty), creating generational wealth.
- **Sylvester Stallone:** Wrote *Rocky* while nearly homeless. He refused to sell the script unless he starred in it. That one film became a franchise and launched a decades-long Hollywood career.

In Sports

Michael Jordan – Cut From His High School Team

Michael Jordan, one of the greatest athletes in history, was famously cut from his high school basketball team. Instead of giving up, he fueled his desire with relentless drive and visualization. His dream wasn't just to play basketball—it became to redefine the sport itself. He manifested not just a career, but six NBA championships, two Olympic gold medals, and a brand that transformed sports and culture globally.

- **Serena & Venus Williams:** Grew up practicing on cracked public tennis courts in Compton, California. With persistence and vision, they not only dominated the tennis world for decades but also broke down cultural barriers in sports and business.
- **Cristiano Ronaldo:** Born into poverty in Portugal, he left home at twelve to pursue football. Today, he's one of the greatest athletes in history with a career spanning decades.
- **Simone Biles:** Adopted out of foster care, she went on to become one of the most decorated gymnasts of all time, redefining what's possible in the sport.

In Literature & Creativity

J.K. Rowling – From Struggling Single Mother to Bestselling Author

Before *Harry Potter*, J.K. Rowling was a single mother living on welfare, writing in cafés while her baby napped. She had no connections, little money, and faced rejection from multiple publishers. Her only resource was her imagination and a deep desire to share her story. Not only did she manifest the dream of becoming a published author, but the series exploded into a global phenomenon—books, films, theme parks, and a cultural legacy she never could have imagined.

- **Maya Angelou:** Overcame poverty, racism, and trauma to become one of the most celebrated authors and poets of the 20th century. Her words continue to empower generations long after her passing.
- **Stephen King:** His first novel *Carrie* was rejected 30 times. He threw it away before his wife retrieved it and encouraged him to try again. It launched his career as one of the best-selling authors in history.
- **Elizabeth Gilbert:** After years of rejection and obscurity, she wrote *Eat, Pray, Love*—which became a global phenomenon and reshaped the conversation about personal transformation.

WHY THEIR MANIFESTATIONS LASTED (AND EXCEEDED EXPECTATIONS)

Looking at stories like Oprah, Tyler Perry, J.K. Rowling, Michael Jordan, and others, there are clear patterns that explain why their manifestations didn't just appear—they lasted and grew bigger than they first imagined.

1. They had a clear inner "why."

Their vision wasn't just about surface-level success (money, fame, recognition). It was rooted in something deeper: storytelling, empowerment, excellence, freedom. That clarity anchored their manifestations, making them resilient to setbacks.

- Oprah wanted to give people a voice.
- Tyler Perry wanted to tell stories of resilience.
- Michael Jordan wanted to prove his worth through excellence.

When your "why" is strong, success has roots.

2. They turned pain into power.

Almost all of them began with hardship: poverty, rejection, trauma, failure. Instead of letting those experiences become blocks, they transformed them into fuel. Their past became part of their foundation, not a weight that pulled them under.

- J.K. Rowling's struggles informed the emotional depth of *Harry Potter*.
- Oprah's childhood trauma fueled her empathy and authenticity.
- Tyler Perry's homelessness became the backdrop for stories that healed others.

They didn't suppress the block—they cleared it by integrating the lesson.

3. They took aligned action (not just intention).

Visualization and belief were part of their process, but action sealed it. They wrote the books, showed up for auditions, practiced endlessly, pitched investors, and persisted when doors slammed shut. They didn't skip Step Three (execution).

- Stallone refused to sell *Rocky* without starring in it.
- Serena & Venus Williams practiced on cracked courts daily.
- Sara Blakely cut up pantyhose and went door-to-door until Spanx caught on.

They moved their energy into form.

4. They reflected and refined.

This is where many people lose manifestations—they stop reflecting. These success stories didn't cling to what didn't work. They evaluated, adjusted, and repeated until the manifestation stabilized and grew.

- Steve Jobs was fired from Apple, but reflection reshaped his vision and brought him back stronger.
- Elon Musk nearly bankrupted Tesla, then pivoted strategy and scaled beyond expectations.
- Oprah reinvented herself multiple times, from local TV to a talk show to network owner.

They didn't just celebrate wins—they used reflection to build on them.

5. They built from alignment, not domination.

Each of them had moments of push and demanded energy, but what lasted came from alignment. They magnetized support, synchronicities, and opportunities because their energy wasn't rooted in fear—it was rooted in vision and trust.

- Rihanna didn't just make music—she aligned her artistry with a global brand identity, creating Fenty.

- Maya Angelou didn't just write—she embodied truth, which sustained her voice across decades.

Alignment made their manifestations scalable and sustainable.

These people didn't have easier paths—they had aligned foundations. Their desires lasted and expanded because they combined **clarity of vision, emotional healing, consistent action, reflection, and alignment.**

Types of Blocks

Before we dive into the *how* of clearing, it's important to understand *what* might be standing in your way, blocks aren't random—they are patterns of energy, emotion, or thought that sit between you and your ability to hold what you've manifested.

These blocks can take many forms:

- **Inherited or Collective Blocks** → Old family patterns, cultural conditioning, or collective fears about money, love, or success. Even if you didn't choose them, they can still shape your results—until you clear them.
- **Emotional Blocks** → Unresolved feelings like disappointment, resentment, jealousy, guilt, or shame. These emotions drain your energy and make it hard to sustain gratitude or fulfillment.
- **Mental Blocks** → Limiting beliefs, perfectionism, self-doubt, or constant overthinking. These keep you trapped in fear or comparison, unable to stabilize success.
- **Physical Blocks** → The body holds memory. Unprocessed stress and emotions can be stored in muscles, fascia, or even the nervous system. Chronic tension, fatigue, or illness may reflect unresolved blocks that anchor you in old patterns. Until they are released, these physical imprints can prevent you from fully embodying and holding new manifestations.
- **Conflict of Manifestation** → Sometimes, the block isn't yours alone. If other people's desires or actions intersect with your manifestation, the energies can tangle and create resistance.
- **Energetic Blocks** → Heaviness in the body, cords of attachment, misaligned frequencies, or simply carrying energy that isn't yours. These weaken your foundation and make your manifestations feel unstable.

The key to remember is this: **blocks don't mean you failed.** They are not signs to abandon your dream. They are invitations to refine, heal, and strengthen your foundation. Every block, once cleared, frees energy that makes your manifestation stronger, steadier, and longer-lasting.

Identify the Block

Before you can clear what's holding you back, you have to name it. Manifestations don't slip away because the desire was wrong—they slip because unresolved blocks weaken the foundation. These blocks show up in different ways: through emotions, thoughts, or energy patterns.

Sometimes the block is obvious: disappointment weighing you down, a limiting belief running in your mind, or tension lodged in your body. Other times, it feels vague, layered, or hidden under numbness—you know something is off, but you can't quite put your finger on it.

That's when you need to let the subconscious speak. Tools like **muscle testing** or a **pendulum** can bypass the overthinking mind and reveal what's really underneath. Your body always holds the truth—it just needs a way to communicate it.

Once the block is identified—whether emotional, mental, or energetic—you can begin clearing it. The desire itself doesn't need fixing. What needs to shift is the interference sitting on top of it. When the block is named, the path to lasting manifestation opens.

WAYS TO IDENTIFY THE BLOCK

Blocks often hide beneath the surface, disguised as "bad luck," procrastination, or repeating cycles. To clear them, you first have to bring them into awareness. Here are different ways to uncover what's really interfering with your manifestation:

1. Muscle Testing (Applied Kinesiology)

The body never lies. By testing muscle strength against statements ("I am ready to hold abundance"), you can reveal where resistance or weakness is hiding.

Want to go deeper?
If you'd like to explore a complete system for uncovering hidden blocks through the body's wisdom, see my book *Secrets of a Healer: Magic of Muscle Testing.* It's a practical guide that teaches you how to use muscle testing to identify subconscious patterns, access clarity, and release resistance—so you can strengthen your foundation and create manifestations that last..
ISBN: 978-0-9783005-3-1

HOW-TO EXAMPLES
OPTION 1: USING MUSCLE TESTING

1. **Ground and Center**
   o Stand tall, feet hip-width apart, arms relaxed at your sides.
   o Take 3 deep breaths, imagining your energy settling into the ground.
2. **Set the Intention**
   o Say quietly: *"I am asking to identify the emotional block that is most ready to be cleared now."*
3. **Choose a Testing Method**
   o **Sway Test:** Stand straight. Ask yes/no questions. Notice if your body sways forward (yes) or back (no).
   o **Finger Lock Test:** Make a circle with thumb and index finger of one hand. Loop the other hand's finger through it. Ask yes/no questions,

then gently try to pull apart. Locked = yes; opens = no.

4. **Ask the Question**
   o Example:
      1. *"What type of block is it? Inherited, Emotional, Mental, Physical, Conflict or Energetic?"*
      2. *"Is the block I am feeling disappointment?"*
   o If "no," continue through other emotions: resentment, jealousy, guilt/shame, or use a broader list (see Emotions Chart).

5. **Confirm Intensity**
   o Ask: *"On a scale of 0–10, is the intensity above 5?"*
   o Narrow down until you get the range. This gives you a clear picture of the charge.

2. Pendulum Testing

A pendulum amplifies the body's micro-movements to answer yes/no questions from the subconscious. It's especially useful when emotions feel vague or layered.

OPTION 2: USING A PENDULUM

1. **Calibrate Your Pendulum**
   o Hold it steady by the chain, let it dangle.
   o Ask: *"Show me yes."* Notice the swing direction.
   o Ask: *"Show me no."* Notice the difference.

2. **Set the Intention**
   o *"I am asking to identify the emotional block that is most ready to be cleared now."*

3. **Ask the Question**
   o *"Is the primary block disappointment?"*
   o Move through possible emotions until you get a "yes."

4. **Check Intensity**
   o *"Is the intensity above 5/10?"* Narrow it down until you get the number.

3. Hypnosis or Guided Regression

Hypnosis helps bypass the conscious mind to uncover root beliefs, traumas, or patterns lodged in the subconscious. This can reveal why manifestations collapse even when surface-level actions seem aligned.

Want to go deeper?
If you're curious about working directly with the subconscious to uncover and clear hidden blocks, explore my book *Secrets of a Healer: Magic of Hypnotherapy.* It walks you through how hypnotherapy can reprogram limiting beliefs, release stored emotions, and create lasting change—helping your manifestations stay steady and aligned.
ISBN: 978-0-9783005-9-3

4. AuricIons Release Method

This nine-step process works through grounding, scanning, extraction, and rebalancing to identify and dissolve stuck energy in the auric field. Often, the block is energetic residue from past experiences that hasn't been integrated.

Want to go deeper?
If you feel called to learn a complete, structured method for clearing blocks at the energetic and emotional level, explore my book *AuricIons: Unlocking Subconscious Healing Through Quantum Medicine.* It's a step-by-step guide to identifying, releasing, and integrating energy, ensuring your manifestations remain strong and sustainable. ISBN: 978-1-990062-49-0

5. Journaling with Prompts

Free-writing can surface hidden beliefs. Prompts like *"What am I afraid will happen if I succeed?"* or *"What pattern keeps repeating?"* often reveal the block in plain words.

6. Therapy or Coaching Dialogue

Sometimes blocks are easier to spot when reflected back by someone else. A skilled coach or therapist can notice repeating stories, excuses, or fears that you don't see in yourself.

7. Dreamwork

The subconscious often communicates through dreams. Recurring images of being chased, blocked, or unprepared may reflect emotional or mental blocks needing attention.

8. Body Awareness (Somatic Scanning)

Tension in the gut, tightness in the chest, or heaviness in the shoulders often points to unresolved emotional blocks. The body becomes the map to where energy is stuck.

9. Meditation & Stillness

When you quiet the mind, hidden fears or beliefs often rise to the surface. Blocks that seemed invisible become clear in the space silence creates.

10. Trusted Intuitive Guidance

Whether through your own intuition, a trusted mentor, or a spiritual reader, sometimes a block is easier to identify when seen from an intuitive perspective outside the logical mind.

Key Insight:
Blocks don't hide because they want to stop you—they hide because your system believes it's safer that way. These methods give you ways to bring the block into the light so it can finally be cleared.

What To Do When It Is "Inherited" Blocks

Inherited blocks are patterns you didn't consciously choose—family beliefs, cultural scripts, ancestral wounds, and collective fears that quietly shape what you expect, allow, and keep. They can feel like **invisible ceilings**: you manifest the thing… then an old program pulls you back to the familiar.

Common signs you're dealing with inherited patterns:

- The same struggle repeats across generations (money instability, relationship breakdowns, health anxieties, visibility fears).
- You hit a "set point" and self-correct downward (earn more → spend more; get love → push it away).
- Your inner voice uses family/cultural phrases ("Don't get too big," "Money doesn't grow on trees," "What will people think?").
- Guilt or loyalty conflicts arise when you succeed.
- You feel pressure to keep traditions/roles that don't fit your soul.

You're not broken—you're bonded. Inherited blocks are **loyalty patterns** your nervous system uses to belong and stay safe. We honor the past, then choose differently.

The Garden Metaphor (Lineage Edition)

- **Desire** is the seed.
- **Alignment** is the soil.
- **Action** is the watering.
- **Reflection** is the sunlight.
- **Inherited roots** are the underground network: rich when supportive, strangling when tangled. We don't rip up the whole garden—we **untangle what chokes the seed**.

WAYS TO IDENTIFY INHERITED BLOCKS

1) Genogram & Pattern Mapping (10–20 min)

Draw a simple family map (parents, grandparents, caregivers). Next to each name, bullet key themes: money, love, health, work, visibility, faith, migration/war/collective trauma.

- Circle **repeated themes** (e.g., "start over," "women over-give," "men disappear," "money leaves quickly").
- Star **your theme** where it matches theirs.

Workbook line:
"Across my lineage, I notice repeating patterns of _____."

2) Family Belief Audit

List 10 sentences you heard growing up (explicit or implied). Examples:

- "Good things don't last."
- "It's selfish to want more."
- "Our people don't do that."
- "Hard work = worth."

Label each: **Keep / Update / Release**.

3) Cultural & Collective Scripts

Name the rules your culture/community taught about money, gender roles, success, visibility, spirituality. Ask:

- "What did I have to be to belong?"
- "What did I have to hide to stay safe?"

4) Muscle Testing Across the Line

Hold these statements and test:

- "It's safe to earn more than my family."
- "It's safe to be visibly happy in love."
- "I can keep what I create."
  Weak = likely an inherited block.

5) Symptoms & Set-Point Check

Notice where life "snaps back": income, intimacy, health habits, visibility. That snap is often an inherited thermostat.

WAYS TO HEAL INHERITED BLOCKS AT THE ROOT
1. Loyalty Reframe & Permission Ritual

Why: Inherited blocks often run on *love-loyalty*: "If I thrive, I betray them." This ritual honors your lineage while updating the agreement—so you carry the **strength**, not the **struggle**.

Core Mantra: *Loyalty to love, not to limitation.*

Materials (choose any)

- Paper + pen
- Small bowl of water **or** a candle/fire-safe dish (for release)

- Optional: object/photo representing family/ancestors/culture
- Timer (3–20 minutes)

Safety note: If the process brings up intense memories or trauma, pause and ground (feet on floor, slow exhale). Consider doing the deep version with a practitioner.

Quick Version (3–5 minutes)

1. **Arrive (20–30s)**
   - Sit tall, feet grounded. Inhale 4, exhale 6 (twice).
2. **Name the inherited pattern (30s)**
   - On paper: "In my family we learned: _____."
   - "The cost to me now is: _____."
3. **Honor (30s)**
   - Say aloud: **"To my family/ancestors: I honor your path."**
4. **Reframe (30s)**
   - **"I choose to carry the strength, not the struggle."**
5. **Permission (30s)**
   - Hand on heart: **"Your sacrifices rise in me as freedom. I give myself permission to live the answered prayer."**
6. **Release + Seal (60–90s)**
   - Tear or fold the "struggle" line; dip in water or hold near a candle (safely).
   - Repeat 3×: **"Loyalty to love, not to limitation."**
   - One micro-proof action you'll take today: _____.

Full Version (12–20 minutes)

Step 1 — Ground & Orient (2 min)

- 3 breaths (inhale 4, exhale 6).

- Orient: name 3 things you see, 2 you hear, 1 you feel on skin.
- Intention: *"I'm here to honor my lineage and end patterns that no longer serve."*

Step 2 — Map the Pattern (3–5 min)

Create two columns on paper: **Strengths / Struggles** from your lineage.

- List 3–5 in each.
- Underline the one struggle that blocks you most now.
- Rate its pull 0–10.

Step 3 — Honor & Belonging (1–2 min)

Face the photo/object or simply close your eyes. Say:

- **"To my family/ancestors: I honor your path."**
- (Optional specifics: migrations, losses, sacrifices you're aware of.)

Step 4 — The Reframe (1–2 min)

Read your **Strengths** column aloud. Place a hand on heart.

- **"I choose to carry the strength, not the struggle."**
- Breathe in the strengths; on exhale, imagine setting the struggles down.

Step 5 — Release Ritual (2–4 min)

Write the main struggle on a small slip: *"I must stay small to belong,"* etc.
Choose a release:

- **Water:** submerge and whisper, **"This pattern dissolves and returns to Source."**
- **Fire:** (fire-safe) burn and say, **"This vow is complete."**
- **Earth/Air:** bury or tear and scatter, **"I return this to the earth/air."**

Step 6 — Permission Statements (1–2 min)

Hand on heart/belly:

- **"Your sacrifices rise in me as freedom."**
- **"I give myself permission to live the answered prayer."**
  Repeat 3× slowly. Let your posture rise as you speak.

Step 7 — Install the New Agreement (1–2 min)

Write a clear replacement:

- *"In this family line, it is now safe to be well-paid, well-loved, and well-rested."*
- Read it aloud. Post it where you'll see it.

Step 8 — Micro-Proof (1–2 min)

Choose one concrete act in the next 24 hours that **contradicts** the old pattern:

- Save/transfer $20.
- Publish/share something visible.
- Say a kind "no" to over-giving.
- Book a support session.
  Schedule it now.

Step 9 — Close & Track (1 min)

- Rate the pull again 0–10. Note the shift.
- Seal with the mantra 3×: **"Loyalty to love, not to limitation."**
- Drink water; touch the ground with your palm for 5 seconds.

Deep Version (30–45 minutes) — for layered patterns

Add these expansions to the Full Version:

- **Genogram flash-map (5–10 min):** Sketch parents/grandparents/caregivers; jot money/love/visibility themes by each. Circle repeats.
- **Constellation mini-move (5 min):** Place objects for *You / Goal / Pattern.* Say to Pattern: **"I see you, and I release what isn't mine."** Move *You* closer to *Goal* until your body softens.
- **Ancestor blessing (2 min):** Ask inwardly, *"Who in my line knows how to hold this dream?"* Receive a word/symbol; place it on your altar or desk for 7 days.

Scripts by Theme (use or adapt)

- **Money:**
  - *"To my family: I honor how you stretched every dollar. I choose to keep your resourcefulness— and release fear. Your sacrifices rise in me as freedom to create, keep, and grow wealth with integrity. I give myself permission to be the first to keep what I build."*
- **Love/Visibility:**
  - *"To my line: I honor the ways you stayed safe by staying small. I keep your wisdom and release hiding. I give myself permission to be seen and loved without danger."*

- **Work/Over-responsibility:**
  - *"I honor the ethic that got us here. I keep diligence and release self-erasure. I give myself permission to rest, receive, and lead sustainably."*

Secular / Spiritual Options

- **Secular:** Replace "ancestors" with "family system," "lineage," or "earlier generations."
- **Spiritual:** Invite guides/angels; add Ho'oponopono 4-line prayer after Step 5.

If Guilt Spikes (common)

- Hand to heart, exhale long: **"Different is not disloyal. My thriving honors the line."**
- Add one generosity act that **doesn't** collapse you (gift, call, donation with boundaries).

How You'll Know It Worked

- Guilt softens; breathing deepens; posture opens.
- Set-point rises without snap-back (money held, love received, rest allowed).
- You take the micro-proof with less friction.
- Family pushback feels tolerable—you stay kind *and* clear.

One-Page Worksheet

- Old loyalty sentence:

  _____

- Main struggle I release:

  _____ (0–10 → __)

- Strengths I keep (3):

  _____

- New agreement:
  _____
- Micro-proof (within 24h):
  _____
- Post-ritual pull (0–10): __ Date: /

Close each time with the anchor:
"Loyalty to love, not to limitation."

2. Vow & Oath Release

Why: Unconscious vows ("I'll never be like them," "I'll always stay small") bind outcomes.
How (5 min):

- Write 3 vows you suspect you made.
- Cross each out and replace: "I now release this vow. I choose _____."
- Speak aloud. Tear/burn safely as symbolic closure.

3. Lineage Meditation (Meeting the Strength Keepers)

Why: Heals "I'm alone" and connects you to ancestral resources.
How (7–10 min):

- Sit, breathe. Imagine a long line behind you.
- Ask: "Who in my line knows how to do this?" (keep money, love, joy, health).
- See/feel an ancestor/figure step forward with a gift (word, symbol, feeling).
- Receive it to your heart. Say: "I carry this now."

Journal: "The gift I received was _____. It means I can _____."

4. Systemic Constellations (Solo Mini)

Why: Reveals hidden entanglements (e.g., carrying a grandparent's grief).
How (10 min):

- Place objects for: You, Goal, Hidden Pattern.
- Move them until your body feels more open.
- Say to the pattern: "I see you. I release what isn't mine. I return this with respect."
- Move **You** closer to **Goal**.

5. Money Scripts Reset (for legacy scarcity)

Why: Money beliefs are often inherited.
How:

- Write your top 3 money scripts (from the audit).
- Reframe each into a **keeper** belief + micro-proof.
    - "Money leaves quickly" → "Money circulates and returns. (Last week I saved $40 and it stayed.)"
- Anchor with one weekly action (auto-save, debt plan, money meeting).

6. Cultural Narrative Rewrite

Why: To belong, you may have played small.
How:

- Write a one-page "old role" (the good child, the fixer, the invisible one).
- Write a one-page "chosen role" (the builder, the healer-leader, the joyful one).
- Choose one **behavioral proof** this week that matches the chosen role.

7. Ancestor Letters (Not Sent)

Why: Resolve unfinished business respectfully.
How (10–15 min):
"Dear _____,
I inherited _____ from our line. I honor its purpose.
I choose to end this pattern with me.
I keep your strength—your _____—and release the struggle.
Please bless this change. I will use it to honor our family."
Close with gratitude. Store or release ritually.

8. Body–Lineage Release (Somatic + Statement)

Why: Lineage can sit in muscles/fascia (jaw, diaphragm, psoas).
How (3–5 min):

- Gentle shaking + chest opening.
- Press feet into floor, inhale; exhale with a hiss.
- Speak while exhaling: "I release what is not mine. I keep the love."
- Finish with hands over lower belly: *"I am safe to keep what I create."*

9. Hoʻoponopono (Lineage Edition)

Why: Forgives across generations.
How (2–3 min):
With an ancestor/family system in mind, repeat slowly:
"I'm sorry. Please forgive me. Thank you. I love you."
End with: "I set us all free."

10. Hypnotherapy / Regression for Root Beliefs

Why: Access the subconscious moment a belief "took."
How: Guided session to revisit and re-script early imprints

(yours or symbolic ancestral scenes). Install new permissions: *safe to thrive, safe to keep, safe to be seen.*

11. Community Repair & Witnessing

Why: Some blocks are collective (migration, oppression, war). **How:** Join spaces that name and heal these histories. Share your story; witness others'. Belonging to healing communities updates your nervous system's safety cues.

12. Education as Liberation (Practical Rewrites)

Why: "We didn't know how" becomes "Now we do." **How:** Choose one structural skill your line lacked (financial literacy, contracts, boundaries, fertility care, parenting models). Learn + implement one micro-system this month.

13. Environmental & Symbolic Upgrades

Why: Your space can mirror old scarcity/chaos. **How:**

- Declutter inherited objects that hold pain (keep a photo, release duplicates).
- Add symbols of the **new lineage** (a family mission, shared gratitude jar, a "we keep what we build" plaque).

QUICK IDENTIFY–CLEAR FLOW (Universal, 7 Minutes)

1. **Name the pattern:** "In my family, we ____."
2. **Locate loyalty:** "How does being different feel disloyal?"
3. **Permission phrase:** "I honor you—and I choose freedom."
4. **Body seal:** Hand to heart + belly; 3 breaths.

5. **One proof action today:** tiny step that contradicts the old pattern.
6. **Blessing:** "May this change bless everyone who came before and everyone who comes after."

PROMPTS & SCRIPTS

- "The sentence my family lived by was _____. I choose _____."
- "If I thrive, I fear they will think _____. The truth is _____."
- "The strength my ancestors gave me is _____. I will use it to _____."
- "What would it look like to be the **first** in my line to keep what I create?"

Mantras:

- *I keep the love; I release the limits.*
- *I am the turning point.*
- *My success is our healing.*

COMMON PITFALLS (AND FIXES)

- **Guilt spike after a win** → Textbook loyalty bind. **Fix:** Permission Ritual + one generous act that honors the lineage (donation, family support with boundaries).
- **Family pushback** → Normalize it. **Fix:** "Different, not disrespectful." Hold boundaries kindly, consistently.
- **All-or-nothing urgency** → **Fix:** Micro-proofs weekly. Small consistent shifts rewrite lineage faster than heroic bursts.

HOW YOU'LL KNOW IT'S WORKING

- Set-points rise and hold (income, intimacy, health).
- Guilt fades; gratitude grows.

- Your body feels safer being seen.
- Wins stick—and compound.

One-Page Worksheet (for your workbook)

- Repeating lineage theme:
  _____
- Old loyalty sentence:
  _____
- New permission:
  _____
- Gift I keep from my ancestors:
  _____
- Pattern I release with respect: _____
- Micro-proof this week:
  _____

You don't have to choose between **belonging** and **becoming**.
Honor the past, carry the strengths, and consciously retire the
struggle. When you clear inherited blocks, your manifestation
stops snapping back—**it lasts.**

What To Do When It Is "Emotional" Blocks

Emotions are energy in motion. When they flow freely, they fuel, stabilize, and anchor your manifestations. But when they are ignored, repressed, or left unresolved, they don't disappear—they turn into blocks. These blocks sit on top of your desires, quietly strangling them at the root.

Most people don't lose their manifestations because the dream was wrong. They lose them because the emotional charge wasn't cleared. Disappointment, resentment, jealousy, guilt, or shame build up like static in your field. Instead of supporting your success, these emotions destabilize it—the relationship cracks. The business dries up. The money flows in and then flows right back out.

Think of manifestation like planting a garden.

- **Desire** is the seed.
- **Alignment** is the soil.
- **Action** is the watering.
- **Reflection** is the sunlight.

But if emotional weeds are left unattended, they slowly choke out the roots. The plant may sprout, but it cannot thrive. Without clearing, success feels fragile—and often slips away.

The good news is that emotions are not enemies. They are signals. Every difficult emotion that arises in Step Five is a doorway, pointing to what needs healing or integration. When you meet the emotion directly—naming it, allowing it, and releasing its charge—you free up the energy to sustain what you've created.

In this section, we'll explore the most common emotional blocks that sabotage manifestation—disappointment, resentment, jealousy/comparison, and guilt/shame. For each, you'll receive practical methods to clear the block at the root, so the energy that once drained you can become fuel for growth.

By the end of this section, you'll no longer fear "negative emotions" surfacing during reflection. Instead, you'll see them as invitations—indicators of exactly what to clear so your manifestations not only arrive but last.

Key Insight:
The key to lasting manifestation isn't suppressing or bypassing emotions—it's clearing them. Every method here works by allowing, expressing, reframing, or releasing. When the charge dissolves, alignment is restored, and your foundation becomes unshakable.

COMMON EMOTIONS LIST

Column 1	Column 2	Column 3
Anger	Disappointment	Hope
Frustration	Resentment	Curiosity
Irritation	Jealousy	Inspiration
Rage	Envy	Excitement
Bitterness	Comparison	Joy
Impatience	Guilt	Gratitude
Fear	Shame	Contentment
Anxiety	Embarrassment	Peace

Column 1	Column 2	Column 3
Worry	Regret	Relief
Overwhelm	Insecurity	Trust
Doubt	Loneliness	Love
Helplessness	Betrayal	Compassion
Hopelessness	Abandonment	Forgiveness
Confusion	Powerlessness	Confidence
Sadness	Numbness	Pride (healthy)
Grief	Isolation	Determination
Despair	Rejection	Optimism
Loss	Discouragement	Fulfillment
Hurt	Self-criticism	Calm
Vulnerability	Unworthiness	Empowerment

WAYS TO HEAL EMOTIONAL BLOCKS AT THE
ROOT

1. Awareness & Naming the Emotion

(You don't clear what you haven't accurately named.)

Quick Version (60–90 seconds)

1. **Pause + Posture**
   o Stop what you're doing. Uncross legs, soften jaw, drop shoulders.
2. **Ground**
   o Feel your feet on the floor. Press toes down once.
3. **One Breath**
   o Inhale through nose (count 4), exhale through mouth (count 6).
4. **Locate Sensation**
   o Ask: *"Where is this in my body?"* (chest, throat, gut, head, hands, etc.)
5. **Name It**
   o Say—quietly or in your mind:
     - *"This is **disappointment**."*
     - *"A part of me feels **resentment**."*
     - *"I notice **anxiety** in my chest."*
6. **Separate Self from State**
   o Add: *"I'm noticing this feeling; I am not the feeling."*
7. **Rate It**
   o *"Intensity: 0–10 → it's a 6."* (This helps you track change after clearing.)

Done. You've created space. Now you can choose the right clearing tool.

Deep Version (5–10 minutes)

1. **Set a Container**
   - Timer for 5–10 minutes. Phone on Do Not Disturb.
2. **Orient to Safety**
   - Name 3 things you see, 2 you hear, 1 you feel on your skin. (Signals safety.)
3. **Body Scan** *(head → toes)*
   - Where is tight, hot, heavy, buzzy, numb? Note primary spots.
4. **Name the Top Emotion(s)**
   - Use simple labels: *sad, mad, afraid, ashamed, jealous, disappointed, guilty, lonely, overwhelmed, numb.*
   - If there are layers, name them in order: *"Top: anger; under it: hurt."*
5. **Use Parts Language (optional)**
   - *"A part of me feels angry; another part feels scared."* (Instant de-shaming.)
6. **Write One Sentence**
   - *"Right now I feel [emotion] in my [body area] at [intensity] because [trigger]."*
   - Example: *"Right now I feel resentment in my chest at 7/10 because my effort wasn't acknowledged."*
7. **Validate (2 lines)**
   - *"Of course I feel this. It makes sense because _____."*
   - *"Feeling this doesn't mean anything is wrong with me."*
8. **Breathe It Through (3 rounds)**
   - Inhale to the spot; exhale as if giving the sensation permission to move/soften.
9. **Re-Name (check if it shifted)**
   - Ask: *"What is it now?"* Often the label changes (e.g., anger → hurt at 4/10).

10. **Choose Next Step**

- If the label is **clear**, pick a matching practice (forgiveness, jealousy → inspiration, disappointment → reframe, etc.).
- If still **foggy**, stay with breath + step 6 for one more cycle.

In Public / High-Stakes Moments (30 seconds, silent)

- Micro-breath: in 4, out 6 (twice).
- In your mind: *"This is anxiety, 5/10, throat."*
- Somatic micro-anchor: press thumb and forefinger together; soften shoulders.
- Self-talk: *"Noticing is enough for now."*
- Proceed. (Clear more fully later.)

Prompts & Scripts

- **Label:** *"This is _____." / "A part of me feels _____."*
- **Separate:** *"I am noticing _____; I am not _____."*
- **Permission:** *"It's safe to feel this for one minute."*
- **Curiosity:** *"If this feeling could speak, it would say _____."*

Common Pitfalls (and fixes)

- **Spiraling into the story** (who did what, why it's unfair) → Return to body: *"Where is it? What's the one-word label? Rate 0–10."*
- **Judging the feeling** (*I shouldn't feel this*) → Validation line: *"Of course I feel this; it makes sense because _____."*
- **Numbness** (can't feel anything) → Label the **sensation**: *"I notice numb/heavy/blank in my chest."* → Try temperature/texture words:

warm/cold/tight/pressure.
→ Do 30 seconds of gentle shaking or brisk walk, then relabel.
- **Too many emotions**
  → Pick the **loudest** one first. Clear in layers.

Habit Hooks (to make it automatic)

- **Anchor to triggers:** before opening email, after meetings, before bed.
- **Card on phone/mirror:** *"Name it. Where is it? 0–10."*
- **Bookend practice:** one label in the morning, one at night (journal line).

One-Page Template (for your workbook)

Name it: _____

Where in body: _____

Intensity (0–10): _____

Because: _____

Validation: "Of course I feel this because _____."

After 3 breaths, it is now: _____ (new label/intensity)

Next step (tool I'll use): _____

2. Journaling & Emotional Processing

JOURNALING & EMOTIONAL PROCESSING (HOW TO)

Your rules (always)

1. **No editing.** Write exactly what comes.
2. **Time-box it.** Contain the feeling so it doesn't sprawl.
3. **Pen first, truth first.** Typing is fine, but handwriting helps access emotion.
4. **Name intensity (0–10)** at start and end to see the shift.

A. The 2-Minute Reset (when you're busy)

Goal: vent the charge fast so you can function.

1. **Set timer: 2:00.**
2. **Title:** "What's here now?"
3. **Dump:** Write without stopping. If you stall, repeat: *"What I don't want to admit is…"*
4. **Circle 1 word** that captures the emotion (e.g., *resentment*).
5. **Rate intensity 0–10.** If still ≥6, do one minute of slow exhale (in 4, out 6) and re-rate.

Use this any time you feel hijacked.

B. The 10-Minute Process (daily/after a trigger)

Goal: feel → understand → move.

1. **Set the container (0:30).** Phone on Do Not Disturb; sit tall; three breaths.
2. **Label + locate (0:30).** *"I feel ___ in my ___ at ___/10."*
3. **Free-write (6:00).** Do not pause. Use the prompt that fits (menu below).
4. **Find the need (1:00).** Write: *"What I needed/need now is…"*
5. **One boundary or action (1:00).** *"To honor this, I will…"* (one tiny step).
6. **Close + re-rate (1:00).** *"Right now it's ___/10. Because of this, I now know…"*
7. **Somatic seal (0:30).** Hand on heart + one steady breath.

C. Deep-Dive (20–30 minutes, weekly)

Goal: clear layers and extract wisdom.

1. **Scene set (2:00):** Candle, music optional; intention: *"I'm here to tell the truth and release what's ready."*
2. **Timeline splice (5:00):** Bullet the last week's emotional spikes. Pick the loudest one.
3. **Write the unsent letter (10:00):** Use templates below.
4. **Shadow-to-need (5:00):** *"Under this feeling is the need for ____."*
5. **Integration (5:00):** Three lessons + one promise to self.
6. **Release ritual (2:00):** Tear, tuck away, or (safely) dispose. Drink water.

Prompt Menus (choose 1–2 and go)

Disappointment

- *What did I hope would happen, exactly?*
- *Where did reality serve me anyway?*
- *What does this teach me about what I actually want next?*

Resentment

- *Where did I abandon myself or a boundary?*
- *What felt unfair—and what power can I reclaim now?*
- *If I returned my energy to me, what would change today?*

Jealousy / Comparison

- *What do they mirror about my unclaimed desire?*
- *If this is proof it's possible, what's my next tiny step?*
- *Where can I applaud them and still choose me?*

Guilt / Shame

- *What was I protecting when I chose that?*
- *What did the "then-me" not yet know?*
- *What am I willing to repair—or release—now?*

Anger

- *What value was violated?*
- *What boundary restores integrity?*
- *Where does this anger want movement? (say, write, change)*

Fear / Anxiety

- *What threat does my body think is here?*
- *Worst/best/most likely case? How would I handle each?*
- *What evidence says I'm safer than my fear suggests?*

Unsent Letter Templates (10 minutes)

To a person (not sent):
Dear ___,
What I felt was…
What I needed was…
What I made it mean about me was…
The truth I choose now is…
I release responsibility for… I reclaim responsibility for…
Goodbye to… Hello to…
Signed, me.

To your past self:
I see you, (age/time). You did X to stay safe. Thank you.
Here's what we know now…
I forgive you for… I'm proud of you for…
I'll protect us by…

To Life/Universe:
I'm frustrated about… I'm grateful for…
Teach me how to… Show me the next step for…
I release the timeline. I commit to the practice of…

Seal each letter with one line: *"This is complete for now."* Then store or dispose (safely).

Sentence Stems (when stuck)

- *The part I didn't want to write is...*
- *If I tell the whole truth, it's...*
- *What hurts most is...*
- *What I need and can give myself today is...*

Aftercare (always)

- Drink water.
- A few shoulder rolls or 30 seconds of shaking.
- If intensity stayed ≥7/10, pair with breathwork, movement, or your **Somatic Anchor** and consider support if it persists.

How you'll know it worked

- Intensity drops (even 1–2 points counts).
- More breath/space in your body.
- A clear next step or boundary appears.
- Gratitude becomes available again.

3. Inner Child Work

Many emotional blocks aren't just about the present—they are echoes from the past. Often, when disappointment, resentment, jealousy, or shame flare up, it's not only your adult self reacting. It's a younger version of you—your *inner child*—who still feels unheard, unsafe, or unworthy.

By connecting with and caring for this inner child, you release the old charge and meet the need that was never met. Once that part of you feels safe, the emotional block begins to dissolve.

QUICK GROUNDING (1 MINUTE)

1. Sit comfortably, close your eyes.
2. Place one hand on your heart, one on your belly.
3. Take 3 slow breaths, signaling safety.

Step 1 – Meet Your Inner Child

- Picture yourself at a younger age (choose the age that comes to mind first—don't overthink).
- Notice their expression, posture, and feelings. Are they sad, scared, angry, lonely?

Step 2 – Offer Presence

- Imagine yourself walking up to this younger you.
- Kneel or sit at their level. Look them in the eye.
- Say: *"I see you. I'm here with you now."*
- Let them know they are not alone anymore.

Step 3 – Ask What They Need

- Gently ask: *"What did you need back then that you didn't receive?"*
- Listen for a word, image, or feeling. (Examples: safety, love, approval, freedom, encouragement.)

Step 4 – Give What Was Missing

- If they needed comfort: Imagine hugging them.
- If they needed protection: Stand between them and the threat.
- If they needed encouragement: Say the words out loud—*"You are worthy. You are loved. You are safe to be yourself."*

Step 5 – Integrate the Gift

- Visualize your younger self smiling, softening, or relaxing.
- Imagine them merging into your heart, becoming part of you again—healed, safe, and supported.
- Say: *"I carry you with love. We are whole."*

Journaling Prompt (optional)

- *"My inner child wanted me to know…"*
- *"The words I most needed to hear back then are…"*
- *"The way I will honor this part of me today is…"*

Aftercare

- Drink water or hold something grounding (stone, pillow, warm tea).
- If big emotions arise, combine this practice with your **Journaling & Emotional Processing** or **Somatic Anchor** to stabilize.

Why This Works

When you soothe the child inside who first experienced the wound, the adult no longer has to keep repeating the block. The loop breaks, and the energy once tied up in old pain is freed for alignment and manifestation.

4. Shadow Work / Integration

Your "shadow" is not evil or wrong—it is simply the parts of you you've learned to hide, suppress, or deny. Emotional blocks often sit here, disguised as jealousy, resentment, shame, or anger. Instead of rejecting these emotions, shadow work invites you to explore them with curiosity.

When you ask what the emotion is trying to teach you, it shifts from a block into guidance. Integration is the process of reclaiming that part of yourself and using it as fuel for growth.

Step 1 – Acknowledge the Shadow Emotion

- Pause when a heavy feeling shows up (jealousy, shame, resentment, anger).
- Say: *"This is here. I don't have to like it, but I will listen to it."*

Step 2 – Name Its Voice

- Imagine the emotion as a character or younger version of yourself.
- Give it a voice: *"I'm jealousy, and I'm here to tell you…"*
- Write or speak its message without censorship.

Step 3 – Ask the Shadow Question

- *"What are you trying to show me about what I really want?"*
- *"What part of me have I been disowning or hiding?"*
- *"What need or boundary have I been ignoring?"*

Step 4 – Translate the Message

- Jealousy may reveal a hidden desire: *"I want to be recognized too."*
- Anger may reveal a violated value: *"Fairness matters deeply to me."*
- Shame may reveal a longing: *"I want to feel worthy of love."*

Step 5 – Integrate the Gift

- Affirm: *"I reclaim this part of me."*
- Turn the shadow insight into a guiding statement:
  - *"Jealousy shows me I desire visibility. I now choose aligned ways to create it."*
  - *"Anger shows me I value respect. I now set clear boundaries."*

Step 6 – Anchor It in Action

Choose one small, concrete step that honors the insight.

- If jealousy revealed your desire for expression → post, share, or speak today.
- If resentment revealed over-giving → say "no" once this week.
- If shame revealed unworthiness → do one act of self-care without guilt.

Journaling Prompts

- *"The shadow I resist the most is..."*
- *"What this emotion is trying to teach me is..."*
- *"The part of me I am ready to reclaim is..."*
- *"One action I can take to honor this insight is..."*

Why This Works

Shadow emotions are like locked rooms in your house. Ignoring them doesn't make them disappear—it just keeps part of your energy trapped. By opening the door, listening, and reclaiming what's inside, you become more whole. Integration transforms emotional charge into usable wisdom, turning blocks into bridges.

5. Somatic Release (Body-Based Practices)

Emotions are not only thoughts or feelings—they are **biological events**. When emotions are not expressed, the body stores their charge in muscles, fascia, breath patterns, and the nervous system. Over time, this creates tension, pain, or the sensation of being "stuck."

Somatic release is the process of letting the body do what it naturally knows how to do: discharge energy and return to balance. These practices give your body permission to complete the cycles that got interrupted.

Practice 1 – Shaking / Tremoring

- Stand with feet hip-width apart, knees loose.
- Begin by bouncing gently on your heels.
- Let the shaking spread through your legs, hips, arms, shoulders.
- Shake for 1–2 minutes, making sound if it feels natural.
- Finish by standing still with eyes closed, noticing the difference.

Best for: stress, fear, overwhelm, or when energy feels "stuck" in the body.

Practice 2 – Breathwork

Breath changes chemistry instantly. Use different rhythms depending on what you're clearing.

- **Long Exhale for Anger / Tension**
  - Inhale through the nose (count of 4).
  - Exhale through the mouth (count of 8).
  - Repeat 5–10 cycles.
- **Fast Breath for Anxiety / Restlessness**

- Inhale + exhale quickly through the nose, like a "panting" dog.
- Do for 20–30 seconds, then pause and breathe normally.

Best for: anger, anxiety, nervous energy.

Practice 3 – Stretching / Movement

Target the body parts where emotions often live.

- **Grief / Sadness** → Open the chest. Interlace hands behind your back, lift gently, expand the heart space.
- **Resentment / Stagnation** → Twist the spine. Seated or standing, twist to each side with exhale, visualizing tension leaving.
- **Anger / Frustration** → Stomp feet firmly on the ground. Imagine energy moving down into the earth.

Best for: grief, frustration, resentment, feeling heavy or sluggish.

Practice 4 – Crying / Laughing Release

Crying and laughing are built-in reset buttons for the nervous system.

- Give yourself permission to cry without judgment. Set a timer for 5 minutes if needed.
- Watch a funny video or practice forced laughter until it becomes real (laughter yoga style).
- Both crying and laughing regulate breathing and release tension in the diaphragm.

Best for: grief, shame, helplessness, or when you feel blocked from joy.

How to Use Somatic Release in Daily Life

1. **Notice** where emotion lives in the body (chest, gut, throat, shoulders).
2. **Choose** one release practice that matches your state (anger → stomping; sadness → chest opening; anxiety → fast breathing).
3. **Move** for 1–5 minutes.
4. **Pause** afterward to notice the shift.
5. **Repeat** as needed. Small daily releases prevent buildup.

Reflection Prompt

- *"Where in my body do I most often hold emotion?"*
- *"Which somatic practice gives me the most relief?"*
- *"What would change in my life if I allowed myself to release daily?"*

Why This Works

Somatic practices bypass overthinking. Instead of analyzing emotions endlessly, they let the body resolve them directly. Once the charge is released physically, reflection becomes lighter, and manifestation can stabilize in a clear, open field.

6. Forgiveness Practices

Resentment is one of the heaviest emotional blocks because it keeps you tied to the past. As long as you replay the story of who hurt you or how life was unfair, your energy remains stuck there. Forgiveness isn't about saying what happened was "okay." It's about freeing *yourself* from carrying the weight.

Forgiveness is release. It cuts the cord between you and the pain so you can move forward lighter, clearer, and open to new manifestations.

Practice 1 – The Forgiveness Letter (not sent)

1. Set aside 10–15 minutes in a quiet space.
2. Write: *"Dear [name / situation / younger self],"*
3. Express the truth: *"This is what I felt... This is what hurt... This is what I wished had been different..."*
4. Acknowledge the impact: *"Because of this, I carried resentment, anger, or sadness..."*
5. Choose release: *"I now release this story from my body and mind. I no longer carry this weight."*
6. Close: *"I forgive you. I release you. I set myself free."*
7. End with your signature. Tear it up, burn it safely, or tuck it away.

Practice 2 – Visualization Release

1. Sit comfortably, close your eyes.
2. Picture the person, situation, or younger self in front of you.
3. Surround them in light—golden, white, or whatever color feels healing.
4. Imagine the resentment as a heavy cord between you.
5. With compassion, see the cord dissolve, melt, or turn into light.
6. Say silently or out loud: *"I release this story from my body and mind."*
7. Feel the space it leaves behind fill with love, peace, or calm.

Practice 3 – Spoken Release

When the weight of resentment rises in your body, pause and place a hand on your heart. Whisper:

- *"I release this story from my body and mind."*
- *"I keep the lesson, but I let go of the pain."*
- *"Forgiveness is my freedom."*

Repeat until you feel a softening in your body.

Journaling Prompt

- *"Who or what am I still carrying that drains my energy?"*
- *"What boundary, lesson, or truth do I keep, even as I release the pain?"*
- *"How would my life feel lighter if I forgave this today?"*

Why This Works

Forgiveness dissolves resentment at the root. Instead of replaying the wound, you integrate the lesson and free the energy tied up in bitterness. This lightness opens the channel for gratitude, which stabilizes manifestation and keeps it flowing.

7. Energy Clearing Techniques

Emotions leave energetic imprints. Even after you've processed the story or calmed the mind, the residue can linger in your field—like static electricity that clings. Energy clearing practices remove this residue so your body, mind, and spirit feel light again.

These techniques are quick, intuitive, and can be used anytime you sense heaviness, stickiness, or cords to people and situations draining your energy.

Practice 1 – Visualization Release

How to:

1. Close your eyes and breathe deeply.
2. Imagine the blocked emotion as a **form**—dark smoke, heavy stone, tangled roots, or sludge.
3. With each exhale, see it leaving your body.

- o Smoke drifting upward into the sky.
- o Stones dropping into the earth.
- o Roots dissolving in light.
4. Inhale golden light, filling the space where the heaviness was.
5. Continue until you feel lighter.

Best for: generalized heaviness, sadness, or when you can't name the exact block.

Practice 2 – Cord Dissolution

Energetic cords form when you're emotionally entangled with someone else (past partner, friend, family, colleague). They can drain your energy or keep you looping in the past.

How to:

1. Sit quietly and picture the person in your mind.
2. Notice cords connecting you (commonly at the heart, solar plexus, or throat).
3. Place a hand on the cord and gently pull it out **at the root**, returning it to them with compassion.
4. Fill the space in your body with golden light or love.
5. Say: *"I return your energy to you, and I reclaim mine."*

Note: This is not about cutting someone out of your life. It's about dissolving unhealthy attachments so you can interact with them (or their memory) in freedom.

Practice 3 – Aura Brushing

Your aura (energy field) is like your energetic skin. It can collect residue from stress, other people, or environments. Aura brushing "wipes it clean."

How to:

1. Stand tall, feet grounded.
2. With your hands, sweep downward along the front, sides, and back of your body—about 3–6 inches away from the skin.
3. Brush away tension, as if wiping dust off glass.
4. Shake your hands afterward, imagining the heaviness falling into the earth for recycling.

Best for: after difficult interactions, crowded places, or when you feel drained for no clear reason.

Journaling Prompt

- *"What energy am I still carrying that isn't mine?"*
- *"Where in my life do I need to reclaim my power?"*
- *"What light or intention do I want to fill myself with instead?"*

Why This Works

Energy hygiene is as important as emotional or mental hygiene. By clearing cords, residue, and heaviness, you restore flow and protect your manifestation from being drained or distorted. A clear field = a stable manifestation.

8. Reframing & Cognitive Shifts

Your mind interprets every experience through a story. When that story is negative—*"I failed, I'm behind, I don't deserve this"*—it keeps you stuck in emotional loops and blocks manifestation from stabilizing.

Reframing doesn't deny what happened. It changes the meaning you give it. A cognitive shift transforms a "failure" into a lesson, jealousy into clarity, and guilt into growth. This isn't positive thinking; it's **choosing a more empowering lens** that keeps you aligned instead of stuck.

HOW TO PRACTICE REFRAMING
Step 1 – Catch the Old Story

Notice when you're spinning a thought like:

- *"I always fail."*
- *"They have it, so I can't."*
- *"I don't deserve this."*

Step 2 – Name the Emotion Behind It

- Disappointment → *"It didn't work."*
- Jealousy → *"They have it, I don't."*
- Guilt/Shame → *"I'm wrong for wanting this."*

Step 3 – Ask the Reframe Question

- *"What else could this mean?"*
- *"What lesson or gift is hidden here?"*
- *"How would the confident version of me interpret this?"*

Step 4 – Create the New Frame

Examples:

- **Disappointment → Learning**
  - Old story: *"I failed."*
  - Reframe: *"This didn't fail me; it taught me what's next."*
- **Jealousy → Inspiration**
  - Old story: *"They're ahead of me."*
  - Reframe: *"What I admire in them is proof it's possible for me."*
- **Guilt/Shame → Growth**

o Old story: *"I ruined my chance."*
o Reframe: *"I made a choice then. I choose differently now."*

Step 5 – Anchor with Action

Reframes stick when paired with behavior.

- If disappointment → learning: take one new step informed by the lesson.
- If jealousy → inspiration: try one action your "expanded self" would take.
- If guilt → growth: choose one aligned action that proves you're moving forward.

Journaling Prompts

- *"What old story am I replaying about this situation?"*
- *"What new story would empower me instead?"*
- *"If I believed this new story fully, what action would I take today?"*

Why This Works

Your subconscious acts on the story you feed it. By reframing, you don't erase reality—you **reshape your relationship to it.** Every reframe is a bridge from block to alignment, turning setbacks into stepping stones and keeping your energy steady enough to hold manifestation.

9. Gratitude as an Antidote

Gratitude is one of the fastest ways to shift energy. It doesn't erase emotional blocks, but it **softens their grip** so you can clear them more easily. When you feel resentment, jealousy, or entitlement, your nervous system contracts into fear and scarcity. Gratitude gently reopens it.

Think of gratitude as an antidote: it neutralizes the poison of comparison, bitterness, and lack. From this rebalanced state, you can process and release emotions without getting overwhelmed.

HOW TO PRACTICE GRATITUDE IN THE MIDST OF A BLOCK

Step 1 – Pause and Name the Emotion

- *"I feel resentment."*
- *"I feel jealousy."*
- *"I feel scarcity."*

Step 2 – Anchor in the Present Moment

Take 1–2 slow breaths. Place your hand on your chest or belly. Say:

- *"Even as I feel this, I am safe right now."*

Step 3 – List 3–5 Gratitudes

Write or speak out loud:

- *"I am grateful for…"* (choose anything real and accessible).
- Examples: warm sunlight, a supportive friend, your breath, a recent lesson learned.

Important: The gratitudes don't have to match the emotion. You can be resentful about work *and still grateful* for your morning coffee or your dog's wagging tail.

Step 4 – Add One "In the Midst" Gratitude

Say:

- *"Even while I feel ___, I am grateful for ___."*
- Example: *"Even while I feel jealousy, I am grateful this feeling shows me what I want."*

Step 5 – Notice the Shift

Check in with your body. The emotion may not be gone, but the charge softens. You'll feel more space and less contraction.

Journaling Prompts

- *"Even while I feel ___, I can still be grateful for ___."*
- *"What small things am I overlooking that are actually supporting me?"*
- *"What lesson or growth is hidden inside this emotion that I can appreciate?"*

Why This Works

Gratitude resets the nervous system from fight-or-flight into safety. When you feel safe, your body can process and release emotions instead of clinging to them. Gratitude also shifts focus from what's missing to what's already working, keeping manifestation anchored in abundance rather than lack.

10. Rituals for Release

Sometimes clearing an emotional block requires more than thinking or journaling—it needs a physical, symbolic act that tells your subconscious: *"This is finished. I am free."* Rituals give emotions a place to land and a way to leave.

You don't have to believe in ceremony to benefit. The act of doing something symbolic—burning, burying, washing— creates a sense of closure that the nervous system recognizes.

Practice 1 – Fire Release (burning words)

- Write down everything you feel about the block: the anger, disappointment, jealousy, or guilt. Don't hold back.
- When you're ready, safely burn the paper in a fireproof dish, fireplace, or outdoors.
- As it turns to ash, say: *"I release this story from my body and mind. I set myself free."*
- Bury or scatter the ashes as a sign of completion.

Best for: anger, resentment, grudges.

Practice 2 – Earth Release (burying)

- Choose an object that represents the block (a stone, leaf, twig, or even a note you've written).
- Hold it in your hands, breathe the emotion into it.
- Bury it in the earth, saying: *"I return this to the soil to be transformed."*
- Walk away knowing the earth is composting the heaviness into something new.

Best for: grief, shame, and old stories you've carried for years.

Practice 3 – Water Release (washing away)

- Stand under a shower, soak in a bath, or visit a river/lake/ocean.
- As the water runs over you, imagine it pulling the heaviness off your body.
- Say: *"This weight dissolves and flows away. I am cleansed, renewed, restored."*
- When finished, towel off slowly, feeling lighter.

Best for: disappointment, sadness, or after emotionally draining days.

Practice 4 – Air Release (breath & voice)

- Go outside or near an open window.
- Take a deep inhale, then exhale forcefully, imagining the block leaving with your breath.
- Option: shout, sigh loudly, or use a vocal sound (like a hum or "HA!").
- Repeat until you feel your body soften.

Best for: anxiety, frustration, nervous tension.

Journaling Prompt

- *"If I let this go fully today, what would feel different in my body?"*
- *"Which ritual feels most powerful for me right now— fire, earth, water, or air?"*

Why This Works

Rituals speak the language of the subconscious. They transform abstract emotions into tangible actions, signaling closure at every level—mind, body, and energy. Once the ritual is complete, you no longer carry the block in the same way.

11. Therapeutic Dialogue / Parts Work

THERAPEUTIC DIALOGUE / PARTS WORK

We are not one single voice—we are made of many "parts." A part of you may feel jealous, while another part feels hopeful. One part wants to take a risk, another part wants to stay safe. Emotional blocks often come from parts of you that are scared, unheard, or trying to protect you in clumsy ways.

Using *parts language* turns inner conflict into a conversation instead of a war. It reduces shame ("I shouldn't feel this") and creates space for integration.

Step 1 – Name the Part

- Instead of saying *"I am jealous,"* say: *"A part of me feels jealous."*
- This shifts the feeling from your identity to just one aspect of you.

Step 2 – Externalize It

- Imagine this part as a younger you, a character, or even a symbol (e.g., the jealous part could look like a child left out of a game).
- Give it a seat across from you in your mind's eye or in your journal.

Step 3 – Begin the Dialogue

Ask questions directly:

- *"What do you need right now?"*
- *"What are you afraid will happen if I succeed?"*
- *"How are you trying to protect me?"*

Write or listen for the answers without judgment.

Step 4 – Respond With Compassion

Speak back as your adult, grounded self:

- *"Thank you for trying to keep me safe."*
- *"I hear you. I won't ignore you."*
- *"Here's what I will do to care for you and move us forward."*

Step 5 – Integrate the Part

- Imagine the part relaxing, softening, or merging into your body with ease.
- Say: *"We are on the same team. I carry you with compassion."*

Journaling Prompts

- *"A part of me feels… Another part of me feels…"*
- *"The part that feels scared is afraid of… and needs…"*
- *"The way I can honor this part while still moving forward is…"*

Why This Works

Parts work shows you that no emotion is your enemy. Every part—even jealousy, anger, or fear—is trying to help in its own way. When you listen, thank it, and integrate it, the block dissolves. What felt like resistance becomes wisdom and strength.

12. Breath-Heart Bridging

When emotions run high, the mind often spins and the body contracts. Breath-heart bridging is a simple but powerful way to bring coherence back to your system. By linking breath with the heart, you create a direct channel for release and renewal.

This practice softens emotional intensity, clears heaviness, and replaces it with compassion—toward yourself and others.

HOW TO PRACTICE BREATH-HEART BRIDGING
Step 1 – Position

- Sit or lie down comfortably.
- Place one hand on your belly (just below the navel) and one hand on your heart.

Step 2 – Breathe Into the Belly

- Inhale slowly through the nose, allowing the belly to rise beneath your lower hand.
- This grounds you and signals safety to the nervous system.

Step 3 – Exhale Through the Heart

- Exhale slowly through the mouth or nose.
- Imagine the breath flowing upward and out through your heart space.
- Visualize the blocked emotion leaving on the exhale— like smoke, mist, or weight being released.

Step 4 – Add Compassion on the Inhale

- As you inhale again, imagine drawing compassion, love, or light into your body.
- See this energy filling your chest and spreading through your whole body.

Step 5 – Repeat

- Continue for 6–10 breaths.
- With each cycle:
    - Exhale = release heaviness.
    - Inhale = receive compassion.

Step 6 – Seal the Practice

- Rest both hands on your heart for a moment.
- Whisper to yourself: *"I am safe. I am open. I am whole."*

Journaling Prompt (optional)

- *"The emotion I released was…"*
- *"The compassion I allowed in feels like…"*
- *"What I choose to carry forward is…"*

Why This Works

Breathing is the fastest way to reset your nervous system. By connecting the belly (safety, grounding) and the heart (compassion, expansion), you create balance. This clears emotional charge without overthinking and restores the inner coherence that manifestation depends on.

13. Meditation & Mindfulness

One of the most powerful ways to clear emotional blocks is also the simplest: **observe without judgment.** Most emotions become overwhelming not because of the feeling itself, but because of the resistance around it. The mind says, *"This shouldn't be here. I need to get rid of this now."* That resistance amplifies the charge.

Mindfulness creates space. By noticing an emotion as a passing state—like a cloud drifting across the sky—you stop fusing with it. The emotion can then move through naturally without leaving residue.

HOW TO PRACTICE MEDITATION & MINDFULNESS
Step 1 – Find Stillness

- Sit comfortably with your back supported.
- Close your eyes or soften your gaze.
- Take 3 slow breaths, allowing your body to settle.

Step 2 – Notice the Emotion

- Bring to mind the situation that stirred the block.
- Ask: *"What am I feeling right now?"*
- Notice where it lives in your body (tight chest, heavy gut, tense shoulders).

Step 3 – Observe Without Judgment

- Say to yourself: *"This is sadness."* or *"This is anger."*
- Add: *"This is a passing state. It will move through."*
- Imagine you are watching waves rise and fall on the shore—you don't stop them, you let them move.

Step 4 – Return to the Breath

- Inhale gently, exhale slowly.
- With each breath, notice the feeling shifting: stronger, weaker, moving, dissolving.
- If thoughts pull you away, gently bring attention back to the body and breath.

Step 5 – Close with Awareness

- After 5–10 minutes, notice if the sensation has changed.
- End by placing a hand on your heart and saying: *"I allow emotions to move through me. I am not my feelings; I am the space they pass through."*

Journaling Prompt

- *"The emotion I observed was…"*
- *"When I allowed it, I noticed…"*
- *"This showed me that I can…"*

Why This Works

Mindfulness teaches you that emotions are temporary waves, not permanent truths. By observing without judgment, you release the urge to fight or fix the emotion. This reduces intensity, clears blocks naturally, and helps you stay in alignment with your power.

1-MINUTE MINDFULNESS RESET
Step 1 – Pause (10 seconds)

- Stop what you're doing.
- Soften your shoulders and unclench your jaw.
- Take one slow breath in through the nose, out through the mouth.

Step 2 – Label (15 seconds)

- Silently say: *"I notice ___."*
- Example: *"I notice tension." / "I notice sadness." / "I notice frustration."*
- Then remind yourself: *"This is a passing state. It will move through."*

Step 3 – Anchor in the Body (20 seconds)

- Feel your feet on the floor.
- Press your thumb and forefinger together gently.
- Whisper inside: *"I am here now."*

Step 4 – Breath Reset (15 seconds)

- Inhale for 4.
- Exhale for 6.
- Repeat once or twice.

Closing (Optional)

Smile softly or place a hand briefly on your heart and say: *"I can continue lighter."*

Why It Works

This reset interrupts spirals before they take over. It grounds you, separates you from the emotion, and signals your nervous system to settle—all in under a minute.

14. Sound & Voice Release

Your voice is one of the most direct pathways to release emotion. The human body is designed to heal through sound— crying, laughing, sighing, chanting, and humming are natural ways the nervous system discharges tension. When you give sound to what's inside, the vibration carries it out safely.

Many emotional blocks linger because we silence ourselves. Sound & voice practices return you to expression, freeing trapped energy without words or analysis.

Practice 1 – Humming for Calm

- Sit comfortably, close your eyes.
- Inhale deeply through your nose.
- On the exhale, hum gently, letting your chest and face vibrate.
- Continue for 5–10 breaths.
- Notice how your body softens with the vibration.

Best for: anxiety, restlessness, overthinking.

Practice 2 – Sighing for Release

- Take a deep inhale through the nose.
- Exhale with an exaggerated sigh, dropping your shoulders.
- Repeat 3–5 times.
- Optional: add sound to the sigh (a soft groan or "ahhh").

Best for: disappointment, heaviness, mental fatigue.

Practice 3 – Toning / Chanting

- Choose a sound like "OM," "AH," or even a vowel (A, E, I, O, U).
- Inhale, then sustain the sound on the exhale.
- Focus on where you feel the vibration in your body (chest, throat, head).
- Continue for 2–3 minutes.

Best for: grounding, restoring flow, reconnecting with inner strength.

Practice 4 – Pillow Scream

- Hold a pillow tightly to your face.
- Inhale deeply, then scream, growl, or shout into the pillow.
- Repeat 1–3 times.
- Rest in silence afterward to notice the release.

Best for: anger, frustration, resentment (when energy feels fiery).

Practice 5 – Free Vocal Expression

- Put on music or sit in quiet.
- Let your voice move spontaneously—hums, chants, laughs, sighs, even nonsense syllables.
- Trust the sounds that want to emerge.

Best for: sadness, shame, or when you can't put feelings into words.

Journaling Prompt

- *"When I gave sound to my body, I noticed..."*
- *"The vibration felt strongest in..."*
- *"I felt lighter after releasing the sound because..."*

Why This Works

Sound vibrates through tissues, organs, and the nervous system. It bypasses the mind and shakes loose stored emotion. Whether soft (humming) or loud (screaming), sound is one of the fastest ways to let blocked energy move through you safely.

15. Creative Expression

When words aren't enough, creativity becomes medicine. Painting, dancing, singing, or writing poetry gives your emotions a form outside your body. Once expressed, the energy no longer has to stay trapped inside—it moves, breathes, and transforms into something new.

Creative expression doesn't require talent. You don't need to be an artist, singer, or dancer. The point isn't to create something "good," it's to create something *true.* The canvas, page, or movement becomes a container where the emotion can land and leave.

Practice 1 – Painting / Drawing Release

- Gather simple supplies (paper, markers, paints, pencils).
- Close your eyes, take a breath, and ask: *"What does this emotion look like?"*
- Let your hand move freely—lines, shapes, colors, scribbles.
- When finished, look at the image and ask: *"What is this showing me?"*
- Option: tear, burn, or keep it as a marker of release.

Best for: emotions that feel wordless—grief, confusion, overwhelm.

Practice 2 – Dance / Movement Release

- Put on music that matches your emotion (sad, angry, joyful, soft).
- Let your body move however it wants—stomping, swaying, shaking, spinning.
- Give yourself 5 minutes of uninterrupted movement.
- End with stillness, noticing the shift in your body.

Best for: anger, frustration, stuck energy, or when you feel restless.

Practice 3 – Singing / Sound Release

- Hum, chant, or sing along to music that resonates with your mood.
- Don't worry about pitch—let your voice be raw and honest.
- Allow the sound to grow louder or softer as the emotion shifts.

Best for: sadness, loneliness, longing.

Practice 4 – Writing / Poetry Release

- Set a timer for 10 minutes.
- Begin with: *"If my emotion could speak, it would say..."*
- Let the words flow—poetry, rambling sentences, or even nonsense.
- When finished, read it aloud once, then release it (keep or tear it up).

Best for: clarity, when you need words to witness the emotion.

Journaling Prompt

- *"If I gave my emotion a color, shape, or song, it would be..."*
- *"When I express myself freely, I feel..."*
- *"The message this creative act gave me is..."*

Why This Works

Creativity bypasses the rational mind and gives emotions a channel of expression. Instead of suppressing or overanalyzing, you allow them to move into form and out of your body.

16. Compassion Practice (for self or others)

Compassion is one of the most powerful antidotes to emotional blocks. Where resentment, jealousy, or shame contracts the heart, compassion opens it. Compassion doesn't mean excusing harmful behavior—it means choosing to respond with understanding instead of hardening.

When you offer compassion to yourself, you create safety inside your own body. When you extend compassion outward, you free yourself from the grip of bitterness or comparison. In both directions, compassion restores flow.

Practice 1 – Self-Compassion

1. Place one hand on your heart, the other on your belly.
2. Take 3 slow breaths, grounding into the present.
3. Say softly:
   - *"It's okay to feel this."*
   - *"I am safe to feel this."*
   - *"I can hold myself with kindness."*
4. Stay with the feeling, without rushing to fix it. Let the words soothe your nervous system.

Best for: guilt, shame, self-criticism, disappointment.

Practice 2 – Compassion Toward Others

1. Bring to mind the person tied to your resentment or jealousy.
2. Place your hand on your heart.
3. Say: *"You are human, just as I am human. May you be free from suffering. May I be free from suffering."*
4. Imagine sending them compassion as light, while also surrounding yourself with the same light.
5. When ready, release the image and return to your breath.

Best for: resentment, jealousy, comparison, betrayal wounds.

Practice 3 – Shared Humanity Reminder

- Whisper to yourself: *"This emotion is part of being human. Others have felt this too. I am not broken—I am human."*
- This simple shift replaces isolation with connection, reducing the block's intensity.

Journaling Prompt

- *"If I could speak to myself as I would to a dear friend, I would say..."*
- *"If I could see the other person's humanity, I would remember..."*
- *"Compassion in this situation looks like..."*

Why This Works

Compassion bridges the gap between resistance and release. When you soften toward yourself, you stop fueling shame. When you soften toward others, you stop feeding resentment. Compassion doesn't mean you accept mistreatment—it means you free your energy from bitterness so manifestation can flow.

17. Professional Support

Some emotional blocks are simple—they dissolve with journaling, breathwork, or a ritual of release. Others are heavier, layered, or rooted in old trauma. When the block feels too big to handle alone, the most empowered choice you can make is to seek professional support.

Asking for help is not weakness. It's wisdom. A skilled guide provides perspective, structure, and safety that you may not be able to create for yourself while inside the experience.

When to Seek Support

- You feel stuck in the same cycle despite trying multiple clearing methods.
- The emotion feels overwhelming, intense, or unsafe to face alone.
- Your body responds with panic, dissociation, or shutdown when you try to process.
- The block is tied to unresolved trauma or abuse.

- You sense it's time for deeper transformation than self-work alone can offer.

Types of Professional Support

- **Therapy (Talk or Trauma-Informed):** Works through the root stories, beliefs, and coping patterns.
- **Somatic Experiencing / Body Therapy:** Releases trauma and tension stored in the body.
- **Coaching / Mentorship:** Offers structure, accountability, and a forward-moving path.
- **Hypnotherapy:** Bypasses the conscious mind to reprogram subconscious beliefs.
- **Energy Work (Reiki, healing touch, etc.):** Clears blocks on an energetic and spiritual level.

How to Choose the Right Support

1. **Clarity of Need:** Ask yourself, *"Do I need emotional support, body-based support, or mindset/strategy support?"*
2. **Safe Connection:** Notice if you feel safe, heard, and respected with the practitioner.
3. **Trust Your Intuition:** The right guide feels aligned, even if the work feels challenging.
4. **Start Small:** Try a session or consultation before committing long-term.

Journaling Prompt

- *"Where do I feel too stuck to shift this alone?"*
- *"What kind of support would feel most nourishing right now?"*
- *"How will I know I've found the right person to guide me?"*

Why This Works

Professional support provides a container—someone holding space for you as you go deeper. When you feel safe and supported, your nervous system relaxes enough to release layers that self-work alone cannot touch. With the right guide, healing accelerates, and your power becomes easier to hold with confidence.

EMOTIONAL VS. MENTAL BLOCKS
Emotional Blocks

- **What they are:** Unresolved feelings like disappointment, resentment, guilt, jealousy, grief, or fear.
- **How they show up:** Heavy in the body (chest tightness, gut knots, shoulders tense), reactive in relationships, or sabotaging gratitude and joy.
- **Brain connection:** Emotional blocks primarily live in the **limbic system** (especially the amygdala and hippocampus).
  - The **amygdala** stores fear and emotional charge.
  - The **hippocampus** ties emotions to memory, so old experiences get "replayed" in new situations.
  - When emotions aren't processed, they keep firing the stress response, flooding the body with cortisol and locking you in survival mode.
- **Why they matter for manifestation:** You can attract or create something, but if unresolved emotions are running, they destabilize the result. The nervous system literally interprets success as unsafe.

Mental Blocks

- **What they are:** Patterns of thought, limiting beliefs, self-doubt, perfectionism, and overthinking.

- **How they show up:** Mental loops ("I'm not enough," "It never works for me"), hesitation, procrastination, or constant analyzing without action.
- **Brain connection:** Mental blocks primarily live in the **prefrontal cortex** and the **default mode network (DMN).**
  - The **prefrontal cortex** is responsible for reasoning, decision-making, and planning. When overloaded with limiting beliefs, it gets stuck in analysis paralysis.
  - The **DMN** is the brain's "autopilot network," replaying old stories and self-identity patterns.
- **Why they matter for manifestation:** Mental blocks filter possibility. Even when opportunities appear, the brain dismisses them as unrealistic or unsafe, causing self-sabotage.

Key Difference

- **Emotional blocks = unresolved feelings stored in the body/limbic system.**
- **Mental blocks = limiting thoughts stored in the conscious mind/prefrontal cortex.**

Both are connected: unprocessed emotions often fuel limiting thoughts, and negative thoughts can trigger emotional stress. Together, they create the "static" that makes manifestations slip away.

What To Do When It Is "Mental" Blocks

Mental blocks are often the most invisible—and the most powerful—barriers to manifestation. Unlike emotions, which you can usually feel in your body, mental blocks hide in your thoughts and beliefs. They show up as doubts, overthinking, perfectionism, or stories you've repeated so many times they feel like absolute truth.

These blocks usually form early, shaped by family, culture, or past experiences. You may have absorbed ideas like *"Money is scarce,"* *"I'm not good enough,"* or *"Good things don't last."* Over time, these beliefs settle into your subconscious and act like a thermostat, keeping you from rising beyond what feels "normal" or "safe."

The danger is that the mind is convincing. A thought can sound logical while secretly sabotaging you:

- *"I'll start when I'm more ready."* (perfectionism)
- *"I don't want to get my hopes up."* (fear of disappointment)
- *"I've tried before and failed, so why bother?"* (fear of failure)

The truth is, you don't need to fight your mind—you need to **rewire it.** By bringing mental blocks into awareness, questioning their truth, and replacing them with more empowering patterns, you free up enormous energy for manifestation.

In this section, we'll explore practical ways to heal mental blocks at the root—through awareness, reframing, identity rewiring, visualization, and daily thought hygiene—so your mind becomes a partner in creation rather than an obstacle.

Key Insight

Mental blocks aren't fixed truths—they're **programs**. And all programs can be rewritten. Healing them at the root means:

1. Catch the loop.
2. Question it.
3. Reframe or replace it.
4. Anchor it with action or evidence.

The key is not to fight the mind head-on, but to **interrupt, question, and rewire** it so it supports alignment rather than resistance.

1. Awareness & Thought-Dumping

Mental blocks often thrive in silence. When thoughts swirl endlessly in your head, they feel heavier and more powerful than they really are. Writing them down strips them of their grip—it's like pulling weeds out of the soil so you can see what's really growing.

Thought-dumping is not about neat journaling. It's about emptying your mind onto paper, so you can sort what is fear, what is fact, and what is simply an assumption.

HOW TO PRACTICE
Step 1 – Create the Container

- Set a timer for 5–10 minutes.
- Grab pen and paper (typing is fine, but handwriting slows the mind enough to reveal more truth).

Step 2 – Dump Every Thought

- Write every thought as it comes—without editing or censoring.

- Don't worry about grammar, spelling, or coherence.
- If you stall, write the same thought repeatedly until the next one emerges.

Example:
"I'm not doing enough. I'll never get ahead. Why do I always compare myself? I don't even know if this is possible. I'm tired. I should quit. No, I can't quit. I want more. I'm scared I'll fail."

Step 3 – Label Each Thought

Once everything is on paper, scan back through and label:

- **Fear:** rooted in "what if" thinking, worst-case scenarios, catastrophizing.
- **Fact:** grounded in objective reality (e.g., "I have $200 in my account").
- **Assumption:** conclusions you've jumped to without proof.

Step 4 – Reframe or Release

- For **fear**: ask, *"What is the most likely outcome, not just the worst?"*
- For **assumptions**: ask, *"What evidence do I actually have?"*
- For **facts**: ask, *"What's one empowering action I can take based on this?"*

Step 5 – Close the Practice

- Circle 1–2 thoughts worth keeping (inspired actions, truths).
- Cross out or tear up the rest as a symbolic release.
- End by writing one sentence of clarity: *"The truth I choose to believe is..."*

Journaling Prompts

- *"The loudest thought in my head right now is…"*
- *"If I let this fear go silent, what else might I hear?"*
- *"What truth feels steadier than my assumptions?"*

Why This Works

Your subconscious treats every unchallenged thought as fact. By dumping them out and labeling them, you stop fear and assumption from disguising themselves as truth. What remains is clarity—and clarity clears mental blocks.

2. Cognitive Reframing

A limiting belief is like a distorted lens—it colors everything you see, even if it isn't true. Left unchecked, these beliefs shape your decisions, block opportunities, and sabotage manifestations. Cognitive reframing is the practice of catching these beliefs in the moment and replacing them with balanced truths that support growth.

This is not about lying to yourself with false positivity. It's about finding a more accurate, empowering perspective that allows you to move forward instead of staying stuck.

HOW TO PRACTICE COGNITIVE REFRAMING
Step 1 – Catch the Limiting Belief

- Listen for the automatic thoughts that come up when you try to manifest or move forward.
- Common examples:
  - *"I'm not good enough."*
  - *"I'll always fail."*
  - *"If I succeed, people will leave me."*

Step 2 – Pause and Question It

- Ask: *"Is this belief an absolute truth—or just an old story?"*
- Look for evidence against it: times you did succeed, moments you grew, ways you've been supported.

Step 3 – Create a Balanced Truth

- Replace the old story with something realistic but empowering.
- Examples:
  - Old: *"I'm not good enough."*
  - New: *"I am learning. Progress is proof I am capable."*
  - Old: *"I always fail."*
  - New: *"Every attempt teaches me. Each step brings me closer."*
  - Old: *"If I succeed, people will leave me."*
  - New: *"The right people will celebrate my success with me."*

Step 4 – Reinforce the New Belief

- Say it out loud daily.
- Write it in your journal.
- Pair it with a physical anchor (hand on heart, breath, or posture shift) to make it embodied.

Step 5 – Practice Consistency

- Each time the old belief arises, gently replace it with the new one.
- Over time, the subconscious accepts the new frame as natural.

Journaling Prompts

- *"The belief that stops me most often is…"*
- *"The evidence against this belief is…"*
- *"The new truth I choose to practice is…"*

Why This Works

Your subconscious doesn't care whether a belief is positive or negative—it simply follows repetition. By catching and reframing limiting thoughts, you retrain your mind to expect alignment instead of failure. This unlocks the mental freedom to hold your manifestations with confidence.

3. Affirmations with Evidence

Affirmations alone can sometimes feel hollow—especially when your logical mind doesn't yet believe the words. That's why pairing affirmations with *evidence* creates real transformation. When your mind can see proof of your progress, it begins to accept new truths as reality.

This practice turns "positive thinking" into *neurological reprogramming* by bridging emotion, language, and lived experience. You're not just saying new beliefs—you're teaching your brain to recognize them as *true.*

How to Practice

Step 1 – Choose Your Affirmation
Pick a statement that reflects what you're building, not just what you want.
Examples:
• "I am becoming more confident each day."
• "I can handle challenges with clarity and calm."
• "My work and worth are both valuable."

Step 2 – Find or Create Evidence

After saying your affirmation, immediately back it up with something real:

- "Yesterday, I spoke up in that meeting."
- "I kept my boundary and felt stronger for it."
- "I took time for self-care instead of overworking."

Step 3 – Record and Reinforce

Write both your affirmation and its evidence in your journal. Over time, this builds a visible record of proof your mind can trust. Each example rewires your belief system, turning possibility into confidence.

Step 4 – Repeat with Feeling

Speak your affirmation out loud, feeling the truth of the evidence behind it. Emotion anchors belief deeper than logic alone.

Optional Variations

- **Affirmation Jar:** Write affirmations with real examples on slips of paper. Draw one each morning for reinforcement.
- **Mirror Practice:** Say your affirmation to your reflection, then list one reason it's true today.
- **Voice Note:** Record affirmations and examples in your own voice; listen daily.

Journaling Prompt

- "The affirmation that feels most believable right now is…"
- "The evidence that proves I am growing is…"
- "When I pair words with proof, I notice that…"

Why This Works

The mind resists affirmations it perceives as false, but it relaxes when met with proof. By combining affirmation with evidence, you create cognitive harmony—aligning thought, emotion, and reality. Over time, these micro-moments of truth retrain the brain to default to confidence instead of doubt.

4. Identity Rewire (Self-Concept Shift)

Traditional affirmations can backfire. If you repeat *"I am abundant"* but your mind screams *"No, you're not!"*—the affirmation feels fake, and the resistance gets louder.

The solution is to **anchor affirmations with evidence.** When you link a positive statement to something real you've already experienced, your subconscious relaxes and accepts it as true. This bypasses doubt and builds confidence faster.

HOW TO PRACTICE AFFIRMATIONS WITH EVIDENCE

Step 1 – Choose the Area of Support

Identify the block you're working on:

- Confidence (*"I'm not good enough."*)
- Resilience (*"I can't handle failure."*)
- Worthiness (*"I don't deserve success."*)

Step 2 – Create a Grounded Affirmation

Write an affirmation that speaks to the new truth you want.

- Confidence: *"I am capable."*
- Resilience: *"I can handle challenges."*
- Worthiness: *"I deserve good things."*

Step 3 – Add Real Evidence

Attach proof from your actual life, no matter how small.

- *"I am capable—last week I finished that project on time."*
- *"I can handle challenges—yesterday I solved that unexpected problem."*

- *"I deserve good things—my friends appreciate my presence."*

Step 4 – Speak, Write, and Anchor

- Speak the affirmation out loud daily.
- Write it in your journal.
- Place a hand on your heart or belly as you say it, to embody the truth.

Step 5 – Collect Ongoing Evidence

- Each day, add a new piece of proof.
- The more evidence you stack, the stronger the affirmation becomes.
- Over time, the belief upgrades from "new" to "normal."

Examples

- Old Belief: *"I'm not good at handling stress."*
  - Reframe: *"I handle stress better than I think—I calmed myself during that tough call last week."*
- Old Belief: *"I never follow through."*
  - Reframe: *"I am building consistency—I kept my promise to walk yesterday."*
- Old Belief: *"I don't deserve success."*
  - Reframe: *"I am worthy—I showed up for myself today."*

Journaling Prompt

- *"The affirmation I want to believe is…"*
- *"One piece of evidence I already have for this is…"*
- *"Tomorrow, I will collect more evidence by…"*

Why This Works

The subconscious resists what feels fake. By tying affirmations to evidence, you make them irrefutable. Each repetition rewires the brain not through blind positivity, but through proof. This creates lasting mental alignment that supports manifestation.

5. Belief Mapping (Root Tracing)

Most self-sabotage happens because of **identity conflict.** Your desire is pulling you forward into a bigger version of yourself, but your old self-image is pulling you back to what feels familiar.

If you've always seen yourself as the struggler, the behind-one, or the almost-there-but-not-quite, success will feel unsafe. The subconscious mind runs on what is "normal," and until you rewire that thermostat, it will keep pulling you back down.

Identity rewire is about shifting your self-concept to match the version of you who already lives the manifestation. When your identity and your desire align, results stick—because they feel natural.

HOW TO PRACTICE IDENTITY REWIRE
Step 1 – Define Who You Are Becoming

At the top of a page, write:

- *"Who I Am Becoming."*
- List the qualities, beliefs, and behaviors of your future self.
    - *"I am consistent."*
    - *"I trust myself."*
    - *"I allow success to stay."*
    - *"I make decisions with confidence."*

Step 2 – Anchor With "I Am" Statements

Each morning, choose 1–3 and say them out loud:

- *"I am disciplined enough to finish what I start."*
- *"I am worthy of holding success."*
- *"I am aligned with ease and flow."*

Step 3 – Tie to Small Consistent Actions

The subconscious trusts action more than words. Prove the identity with evidence:

- *"I am disciplined"* → *I kept my promise to walk for 10 minutes today.*
- *"I am consistent"* → *I wrote one sentence in my journal.*
- *"I am confident"* → *I spoke up once in a meeting.*

Step 4 – Rehearse the Future Daily

Visualize your future self already living the manifestation. Step into their posture, tone, and habits for a few breaths. This makes the identity feel embodied, not theoretical.

Step 5 – Upgrade the Thermostat

Every time the old story tries to pull you back, pause and ask:

- *"What would the future me do here?"*
- Then act from that place, even in a small way.

Journaling Prompts

- *"The old identity I'm releasing is..."*
- *"The new identity I am practicing daily is..."*
- *"Today I will prove this by..."*

Why This Works

Your subconscious doesn't fight identity—it protects it. Once you rewire your self-concept, aligned behavior becomes automatic, and manifestation stabilizes as the new "normal." You're no longer forcing change—you're embodying it.

6. Mind-Body Pattern Interrupts

Mental spirals gain momentum the longer they run unchecked. One thought triggers another, which triggers another, until you feel trapped in anxiety, self-doubt, or overthinking. The fastest way to break the cycle is through a **pattern interrupt**—a simple action that jolts your mind and body out of autopilot.

By pairing a physical cue with a conscious command, you reset your nervous system and remind yourself that you always have a choice.

HOW TO PRACTICE
Step 1 – Choose Your Physical Cue

Pick a clear, distinct action that feels slightly unusual:

- Snap your fingers.
- Clap your hands once, loudly.
- Shake out your arms.
- Stomp your foot.
- Tug gently on your earlobe.

Step 2 – Add the Verbal Anchor

As you do the action, say firmly:

- *"Stop. New choice."*
- Or: *"Interrupt. Reset."*
- Or: *"This thought is not me."*

Step 3 – Redirect Immediately

Follow the interrupt with a grounding or aligning action:

- Take one slow, deep breath.
- Place your hand on your heart.
- Repeat an identity-based affirmation (*"I am capable and calm."*).
- Shift into a small constructive action (write one sentence, drink water, step outside).

Step 4 – Repeat As Needed

The first time may feel awkward. But with practice, your subconscious will recognize the cue as a reset signal. Over time, you'll need fewer repeats to break the spiral.

Example in Action

- Thought spiral: *"I'll never get this right… what if I fail… why even try?"*
- Cue: Snap fingers.
- Anchor: *"Stop. New choice."*
- Redirect: Place hand on heart, breathe, say: *"I am learning, and progress proves I'm capable."*

Journaling Prompt

- *"The spiral I most often get caught in is…"*
- *"The pattern interrupt I choose to practice is…"*
- *"The aligned action I will take after the reset is…"*

Why This Works

Your body interrupts what your mind cannot. A sharp, physical action cuts through the trance of spiraling thoughts, while the verbal anchor rewires your brain to choose differently. This quick reset prevents old patterns from gaining traction and keeps you aligned with your desired identity.

7. Scripting / Future Journaling

The subconscious mind doesn't know the difference between imagination and reality. When you repeatedly write about your future as if it already exists, your brain begins to accept it as *normal.* This rewires your mental "thermostat" away from old patterns of doubt and toward alignment with your manifestation.

Scripting is more than wishful thinking. It's a practice that trains your nervous system and beliefs to feel safe in the new reality—so when opportunities arrive, you recognize and hold them instead of sabotaging.

HOW TO PRACTICE FUTURE JOURNALING
Step 1 – Set the Scene

- Choose a quiet moment (morning or before bed works best).
- Open your journal to a blank page.
- Title it: *"My Life Now"* or *"A Day in My Aligned Future."*

Step 2 – Write it in the Present Tense

- Describe your life as if you are already living it.
- Example: *"Today I woke up grateful in my new home. I made coffee and stepped onto the balcony, watching the sunrise with peace in my heart."*

Step 3 – Engage the Senses

- Add details that your body can feel:
  - What do you see?
  - What do you hear?

- o What do you smell, taste, or touch?
- Example: *"The sunlight warmed my skin, and the scent of fresh flowers filled the room."*

Step 4 – Anchor Emotions

- Infuse your writing with how it feels.
- Example: *"I feel proud of how aligned and consistent I've become. I feel grateful for the freedom this new chapter brings."*

Step 5 – Repeat Daily (Short or Long)

- Some days write a full page. Other days just a few sentences.
- Consistency matters more than length—the repetition trains your subconscious.

Example Journal Entry

"Today I woke up in total peace. I opened the curtains and the morning light filled my bedroom, a space that feels so safe and beautiful. I walked into my kitchen, made tea, and checked messages from clients who value and respect me. I smiled because my work feels meaningful, and I love the balance in my life. I am thriving, loved, and free."

Journaling Prompts

- *"What does a perfect day in my future life look like?"*
- *"How do I feel in this version of myself?"*
- *"What small action today aligns me with that future?"*

Why This Works

Future journaling rewires your brain to treat your desired reality as familiar, reducing resistance. The more normal the vision feels, the less sabotage occurs.

8. Visualization with Emotional Encoding

Visualization is a powerful tool because the brain responds to imagined experiences almost the same way it responds to real ones. But the secret isn't just the image—it's the **emotion** you pair with it.

When you anchor your vision in gratitude, joy, or pride, the subconscious receives it as truth. The image becomes emotionally encoded—etched into memory like a real experience. This reduces resistance and makes your desired future feel believable, safe, and attainable.

HOW TO PRACTICE
Step 1 – Settle In

- Sit or lie down comfortably, close your eyes.
- Take 3 deep breaths, releasing tension on each exhale.

Step 2 – Build the Image

- Picture your desired reality as vividly as possible.
- What do you see? Where are you? Who is with you?
- Add sensory detail: sounds, textures, scents, tastes.

Step 3 – Step Into It

- Imagine you are *inside* the vision, not watching it.
- Look through your own eyes, as if it's happening right now.
- Move around in the scene—walk, touch, breathe it in.

Step 4 – Anchor the Emotion

- Ask: *"If this were real, how would I feel?"*
- Let gratitude, joy, pride, or freedom rise in your body.
- Breathe the emotion into your chest, expanding it with each inhale.

Step 5 – Lock It In

- Pair the image and the emotion with a physical cue:
  - Hand on heart.
  - Smile.
  - A whispered phrase: *"It is done."*
- This signals the subconscious to store the vision as reality.

Step 6 – Return Gently

- Take one more deep breath.
- Open your eyes slowly, carrying the emotion into the present moment.

Example

- Image: Standing in your dream home, sunlight streaming in.
- Emotion: Gratitude and pride for creating stability.
- Anchor: Hand on heart, whispering *"I built this with love."*

Journaling Prompt

- *"When I stepped into my vision, I felt…"*
- *"The emotion I want to carry forward into today is…"*
- *"My body knows this vision is safe because…"*

Why This Works

Visualization alone can feel like fantasy. Visualization *with emotional encoding* convinces the subconscious it's real.

9. Worst-Case Scenario Mapping

Fear is often scarier when it's undefined. The mind spins with "what ifs" but rarely names them clearly. By mapping out the worst, the best, and the likely scenarios, you strip fear of its power. What once felt overwhelming becomes something you can plan for, respond to, or even embrace.

This exercise shifts fear from an endless spiral into a grounded perspective.

HOW TO PRACTICE
Step 1 – Name the Fear

- Write the situation you feel stuck in.
- Example: *"Launching my business."*

Step 2 – Map the Worst Case

- Ask: *"What's the absolute worst that could happen?"*
- Write it down in detail, even if it feels dramatic.
- Example: *"No one buys, I feel embarrassed, I waste money."*

Step 3 – Plan the Response

- Ask: *"If that happened, how would I handle it?"*
- Example: *"I'd adjust my offer, ask for feedback, get part-time work if needed."*
- Realize: even worst-case scenarios are survivable.

Step 4 – Map the Best Case

- Ask: *"What's the absolute best that could happen?"*
- Example: *"Clients sign up quickly, I gain confidence, I grow a sustainable business."*
- Let yourself feel the possibility fully.

Step 5 – Identify the Most Likely Case

- Ask: *"What outcome is most realistic based on my effort?"*
- Example: *"Some people buy, some don't. I learn what works, adjust, and grow."*

Step 6 – Compare & Reset

- Notice how the likely scenario is almost never as bad as the worst case.
- Close by writing: *"I can handle challenges, and I am open to the best."*

Example in Practice

- **Fear:** "What if my relationship ends?"
- **Worst Case:** "I'm heartbroken and lonely."
- **Response:** "I'd grieve, lean on friends, and rebuild over time."
- **Best Case:** "We grow stronger and deepen our bond."
- **Likely Case:** "We'll have challenges, but work through most of them."

Journaling Prompts

- *"The fear I am mapping is…"*
- *"The worst case is…"*
- *"If it happens, I can handle it by…"*
- *"The best case is…"*

- *"The most likely case is…"*

Why This Works

Fear shrinks in the face of clarity. When you name the worst case, your nervous system calms because it sees a plan. When you name the best case, you give yourself hope.

10. Question the Block (Inquiry)

Mental blocks often take the form of rigid beliefs: *"I'm not good enough," "I'll always struggle," "It's too late for me."* These statements feel like facts, but in reality they're stories—often inherited, outdated, or unexamined.

Inquiry is the practice of gently questioning these beliefs until they loosen their grip. By asking the right questions, you weaken the block and invite new truths to emerge.

HOW TO PRACTICE
Step 1 – Identify the Belief

Write down one thought that feels heavy, discouraging, or limiting.

- Example: *"I'll never succeed at this."*

Step 2 – Ask Key Questions

Work through each one in writing or out loud:

1. **Is this true?**
    o Can I absolutely know it's true in all cases, for all time?
2. **Who told me this?**
    o Did I learn it from family, culture, teachers, or past failures?

       ○ Is it actually *my* belief, or one I borrowed?
3. **What's the cost of keeping it?**
       ○ How does this belief affect my choices, confidence, relationships, energy?
4. **What else could be true?**
       ○ Is there evidence that points to a different, more empowering story?
       ○ What would I choose to believe if I were free to rewrite it?

Step 3 – Create a New Possibility Statement

Rewrite the belief in a way that opens space instead of closing it.

- Old: *"I'll never succeed at this."*
- New: *"I am learning, and success is a process. Many people before me started where I am."*

Step 4 – Anchor the Shift

- Speak the new belief out loud.
- Pair it with a breath, gesture, or affirmation.
- Return to it daily until it feels natural.

Example in Action

- **Belief:** *"I'm too old to start."*
- **Is this true?** Not necessarily—plenty of people succeed later in life.
- **Who told me this?** Family patterns, cultural narratives.
- **What's the cost?** I stop trying and shrink from opportunities.
- **What else could be true?** My age gives me wisdom, perspective, and resilience.
- **New belief:** *"I have the perfect experience and timing to begin now."*

Journaling Prompts

- *"The belief that blocks me is…"*
- *"When I ask if it's true, I realize…"*
- *"If I let this belief go, I would feel…"*
- *"A new belief I'm willing to practice is…"*

Why This Works

Rigid beliefs survive because they're rarely questioned. Inquiry shines light on them, showing they're not absolute facts but outdated stories. Once the belief loosens, space opens for possibility—and with space, manifestation can finally take root.

11. Daily Mental Decluttering

Mental clutter is like leaving every browser tab open in your mind. Worries, doubts, and unfinished thoughts pile up until you feel restless, scattered, or drained. Over time, this buildup creates a constant hum of background noise that blocks clarity and focus.

Daily mental decluttering is a short, intentional practice that lets you "close the tabs" each evening. By writing thoughts down and releasing them, you signal to your mind that it doesn't need to hold everything overnight. This clears space for rest, repair, and fresh energy in the morning.

HOW TO PRACTICE
Step 1 – Create the Container

- Set aside 5 minutes before bed.
- Keep a dedicated notebook or journal just for this practice.

Step 2 – Dump It All Out

- Write every worry, doubt, task, or unfinished thought circling in your mind.
- Don't edit—just empty it all onto the page.
- Example: *"I forgot to call Sarah. I don't know if my project will succeed. What if tomorrow feels overwhelming again?"*

Step 3 – Declare Release

- When the timer goes off, close the notebook.
- Say out loud: *"These don't run my night. My mind can rest now."*

Step 4 – Transition to Rest

- Take one slow breath with your hand on your heart.
- Imagine leaving the notebook on a shelf in your mind. The thoughts are "stored" safely—you don't need to carry them into sleep.

Example Page

"Unfinished tasks: call bank, email John.
Worries: what if the launch fails, what if I don't have enough energy.
Doubts: am I really cut out for this? What if I let people down?"

(Notebook closed, mind released.)

Journaling Prompt (Optional Expansion)

- *"If I didn't carry these thoughts tonight, I could rest in…"*
- *"The one thought I choose to keep is…"*

Why This Works

The brain relaxes when it knows thoughts are recorded. By clearing mental clutter daily, you prevent buildup, improve sleep, and create space for reflection and inspiration. This simple ritual resets your mind so manifestation energy flows more freely.

12. Replace Perfectionism with Progress Tracking

Perfectionism often disguises itself as "high standards." In truth, it's a mental block rooted in fear of failure, judgment, or not being enough. Perfectionism keeps you stuck by setting the bar so high that nothing ever feels good enough.

The antidote is **progress tracking.** When you celebrate small, imperfect wins, you retrain your mind to value growth over flawlessness. Progress builds momentum, confidence, and self-trust—the very qualities manifestation thrives on.

HOW TO PRACTICE
Step 1 – Recognize the Perfectionism Trap

Common thoughts:

- *"It's not ready yet."*
- *"If it's not perfect, I'll fail."*
- *"I'll start when I know everything."*

Notice how these thoughts delay action or drain joy from what you've already done.

Step 2 – Start a Progress Journal

- Dedicate a notebook, digital document, or app to track your daily wins.

- Each evening, write down 3 things you did—no matter how small.
    - *"I sent one email."*
    - *"I walked for 10 minutes."*
    - *"I wrote one paragraph."*

Step 3 – Reframe "Not Enough" Into Evidence

- Instead of asking, *"Was it perfect?"* ask: *"What progress did I make today?"*
- Over time, you'll see proof that you are moving forward consistently.

Step 4 – Celebrate Imperfect Wins

- Circle or highlight one small action each day that felt meaningful.
- Say out loud: *"I am stronger because of this."*
- Train your nervous system to associate progress with success.

Step 5 – Review Weekly

- At the end of each week, flip back through your entries.
- Notice the accumulation of small wins—you'll see you're further along than you thought.

Example Journal Entry

- *"I recorded 2 minutes of video, even though it wasn't perfect."*
- *"I tried a new recipe."*
- *"I asked for help instead of pretending I had it handled."*

Journaling Prompts

- *"Perfectionism tells me I need to…"*
- *"Progress shows me I already…"*
- *"One imperfect step I can take today is…"*

Why This Works

Perfectionism focuses on the gap between where you are and where you think you should be. Progress tracking focuses on the bridge you're already building. By rewiring your brain to value action over flawlessness, you replace paralysis with momentum—and momentum creates manifestation.

13. Anchored Mantras

Words are powerful, but when paired with breath or movement, they become anchors. Anchored mantras are short, simple phrases you repeat while linking them to a physical cue—like breathing or placing your hand on your heart.

This combination interrupts looping thoughts, calms the nervous system, and rewires the subconscious. Instead of spinning in "what ifs," your mind receives a clear, embodied signal of safety and alignment.

HOW TO PRACTICE
Step 1 – Choose a Mantra

Pick a phrase that speaks to the block you want to clear:

- For doubt → *"I trust."*
- For control → *"I release."*
- For fear → *"I am safe."*
- For worthiness → *"I deserve this."*

Step 2 – Pair With Breath or Gesture

- **Breath Anchor:**
  - Inhale: *"I trust."*
  - Exhale: *"I release."*
- **Heart Anchor:**
  - Place a hand on your chest and whisper: *"I am safe to succeed."*
- **Grounding Anchor:**
  - Stand firmly, hands on thighs: *"I am here. I am steady."*

Step 3 – Repeat in Rhythm

- Say the mantra 5–10 times, syncing it with your breath or movement.
- Let the rhythm carry you into calm focus.

Step 4 – Use in the Moment

- Anytime mental chatter rises, pause and return to your anchor.
- Even 30 seconds of mantra + breath can reset your state.

Example Anchored Mantras

- Inhale: *"I choose ease."* → Exhale: *"I let go."*
- Hand on chest: *"I am safe to feel this."*
- Clap once, then say: *"New choice."*
- Walk with rhythm: Step → *"I am worthy."* Step → *"I keep going."*

Journaling Prompt

- *"The mental loop I want to interrupt is…"*
- *"The mantra that brings me peace is…"*
- *"The anchor I will use (breath, heart, grounding) is…"*

Why This Works

Mantras by themselves can feel flat. Anchoring them with breath or gesture engages both the body and subconscious, creating a whole-system reset. Over time, your mind associates the anchor with safety and clarity, breaking loops faster and helping manifestation stabilize.

14. Reduce Input, Increase Silence

Much of what we call *overthinking* isn't actually thinking—it's noise. With constant input from social media, news, podcasts, and other people's opinions, the mind becomes overloaded. This creates static that drowns out your inner voice and blocks clarity.

Reducing input and increasing silence is like clearing a cluttered desk before starting important work. When you make space, your intuition and creativity rise naturally. Silence doesn't mean emptiness—it means access to your deepest clarity.

HOW TO PRACTICE
Step 1 – Audit Your Inputs

- Notice what drains vs. nourishes your mental energy.
- Common drains: endless scrolling, news cycles, gossip, constant notifications.
- Write a quick list: *"Where am I overfeeding my mind?"*

Step 2 – Create Boundaries

- Limit or remove 1–2 draining inputs (e.g., delete one app, stop checking news before bed).
- Replace with nourishing alternatives (music, a walk, a book that uplifts you).

Step 3 – Schedule Silence

- Commit to at least 10 minutes of silence daily.
- Options: sit quietly with no phone, walk without earbuds, or drink tea in stillness.
- The goal isn't to "do silence perfectly"—it's to give your brain space to breathe.

Step 4 – Listen for Your Inner Voice

- In silence, notice what arises: feelings, insights, ideas.
- Write them down if needed, but don't force. Just receive.

Step 5 – Expand Over Time

- Once 10 minutes feels natural, stretch it to 20–30 minutes weekly.
- Consider a "digital detox day" once a month to fully reset your nervous system.

Example Daily Ritual

- Morning: no phone for the first 15 minutes. Sit in silence with a glass of water.
- Afternoon: 5-minute silent walk.
- Evening: turn off screens 30 minutes before bed; sit quietly with journal nearby.

Journaling Prompt

- *"What inputs clutter my mind the most?"*
- *"When I allow silence, I notice…"*
- *"What truth inside me becomes clearer when I reduce noise?"*

Why This Works

Manifestation thrives on clarity, but clarity can't grow in static. Reducing external noise and adding daily silence restores balance to your nervous system and reconnects you with inner authority. In the quiet, blocks lose power, and guidance becomes audible.

15. Rehearse Success

Self-doubt thrives on mental rehearsal of failure. Before an interview, you imagine stumbling. Before a conversation, you picture rejection. Before a project, you see yourself overwhelmed. The brain doesn't just predict failure—it practices it.

To break this cycle, you flip the script. Instead of rehearsing failure, you **rehearse success.** By visualizing yourself handling a challenge smoothly, your brain builds a memory of competence. This strengthens neural pathways for confidence and primes you to act with calm clarity in real life.

HOW TO PRACTICE
Step 1 – Choose One Specific Action

Each morning, pick one task or challenge for the day.

- Example: sending an email, giving feedback, recording a video, making a call.

Step 2 – Close Your Eyes & Imagine It

- See yourself doing the action step by step.
- Imagine your posture, tone, words, and energy.

Step 3 – Add Sensory Detail

- How does your body feel when you succeed? Relaxed shoulders? Steady breath?
- What do you hear, see, or feel in the successful version?

Step 4 – Anchor the Emotion

- Let pride, calm, or joy rise in your body.
- Breathe into that emotion until it feels familiar.

Step 5 – Repeat Daily

- Spend 1–2 minutes each morning rehearsing.
- Over time, your brain builds a "confidence memory bank" that becomes second nature.

Example

- Task: "Presenting in a team meeting."
- Visualization: "I stand tall, speak clearly, and my colleagues nod with interest."
- Emotion: pride + ease.
- Anchor: smile, inhale confidence, exhale calm.

Journaling Prompt

- *"The task I rehearsed today was…"*
- *"The version of me who succeeded looked/acted like…"*
- *"After rehearsal, I feel more…"*

Why This Works

The brain doesn't fully distinguish between imagined and real experiences. By rehearsing success instead of failure, you train your subconscious to expect things to go well. This reduces anxiety, builds confidence, and keeps you aligned with your future self.

16. Professional Support

Some mental blocks dissolve quickly with journaling, reframing, or affirmations. Others feel stubborn—like knots that tighten the more you pull. When a belief is deeply rooted in trauma, identity, or years of conditioning, it often requires the presence of another mind and heart to help unhook it.

Seeking professional support isn't a weakness—it's a strategy. Just as athletes work with coaches, and musicians work with mentors, your inner life sometimes needs a trained guide to help you shift patterns faster and more safely than you can alone.

OPTIONS FOR MENTAL SUPPORT

- **Coaching**
  Helps you clarify goals, see blind spots, and hold accountability. Coaches challenge distorted thought loops and redirect you toward empowered action.
- **CBT (Cognitive-Behavioral Therapy)**
  Focuses on identifying and reframing harmful thought patterns. Especially effective for anxiety, depression, and rigid negative self-talk.
- **Hypnosis / Hypnotherapy**
  Works with the subconscious directly to rewrite limiting beliefs, habits, and associations that conscious effort alone can't touch.
- **Mentorship**
  Provides lived wisdom and external perspective. A mentor often helps you see possibilities beyond your current self-concept.

When to Seek Support

- You notice the same thought loop returning no matter how much self-work you do.
- The belief feels overwhelming, paralyzing, or linked to old trauma.
- You're unsure how to separate truth from distortion in your own mind.
- You've made progress but feel stuck at a ceiling you can't break through alone.

Journaling Prompt

- *"The belief that feels too big for me to shift alone is…"*
- *"The type of support I'm most curious about is…"*
- *"What would open up for me if I released this belief with guidance?"*

Why This Works

Mental blocks thrive in isolation. Professional support brings perspective, tools, and accountability that speed up breakthroughs. With a guide, you don't just fight the old belief—you replace it with a stronger, more stable foundation.

What To Do When It Is "Physical" Blocks

Physical blocks are the **body's backlog**—tension, pain, fatigue, and dysregulation that make it hard to *hold* what you've manifested. They're not "just in your head." The body stores unfinished stress cycles in muscles, fascia, breath patterns, and the nervous system. When your system is over-taxed, success feels heavy, visibility feels unsafe, and momentum fizzles.

Key Insight:
Physical symptoms are *messages*, not enemies. When you clear the load in the body, desires stop slipping away because your system can finally sustain the energy of the life you're creating.

COMMON SIGNS YOU'RE FACING A PHYSICAL BLOCK

- **Chronic tight zones:** jaw/neck (unspoken truths), chest/diaphragm (grief, pressure), psoas/hips (fight–flight–freeze), low back (support).
- **Breath holds:** frequent sighing, shallow upper-chest breathing, yawning without relief.
- **Energy crashes:** 2–4 PM slumps, wired-and-tired nights, "goal hangovers" after big pushes.
- **Stress chemistry on loop:** clenched teeth, cold hands/feet, digestive flips, headaches.
- **Set-point backlash:** you level up… then get sick, exhausted, or injured and slide back.

WHY PHYSICAL BLOCKS MAKE SUCCESS SLIP

Manifestation increases *load*: more responsibility, visibility, receiving, coordination. If your tissues, breath, sleep, and nervous system are already near capacity, the "new" can't anchor. The body protects you by **down-regulating**—fatigue, pain, procrastination—until you lower the demand or raise your capacity. Our work: raise capacity.

WAYS TO IDENTIFY PHYSICAL BLOCKS AT THE ROOT

1) 3-Zone Scan (90 seconds)

- **Jaw/Neck/Shoulders:** clench, tight SCMs, computer hunch?
- **Ribs/Diaphragm:** shallow breath, chest pressure, frequent sighs?
- **Belly/Psoas/Hips:** knot in gut, tight hip flexors, restless legs?

Circle the loudest zone. That's your "entry point."

2) Breath Pattern Check

Place one hand on chest, one on belly. Inhale.

- Belly rises first? **Regulated trend.**
- Chest/shoulders lift first? **Stress trend.**

3) Tension Timeline

List recent spikes (launch, conflict, travel, grief). Note which body area flared after each spike. Patterns reveal the root.

4) Movement Audit

Last 7 days: hours seated, steps/day, stretching minutes. Under-moving and over-moving both lock blocks.

5) Recovery Markers

- Morning energy 0–10
- Sleep quality 0–10

- HR spikes after minor stress? (body says "overdrawn")
Low scores = capacity issue, not willpower.

Gentle disclaimer: Persistent or severe symptoms deserve medical evaluation. Clearing blocks complements—not replaces—appropriate care.

WAYS TO HEAL PHYSICAL BLOCKS AT THE ROOT

1. Breath Mechanics Reset (Coherence Breath, 5 minutes)

Why: Breath is the remote control for your nervous system.
How: Inhale 4–5 counts, exhale 6–7 counts, through nose if possible.
Cues: Soften jaw, widen lower ribs 360°, exhale slower than inhale.
When: First thing AM, pre-meeting, pre-sleep.

2. Vagus Nerve Toners (2–3 minutes)

- **Humming/Toning:** 5–10 long hums (vibration = ventral vagal).
- **Cold Splash:** cool water on face/neck 10–20s.
- **Gargle:** 30–60s until eyes water slightly (true tone).
Use before tough conversations or receiving moments.

3. Fascia Floss (3–6 minutes total)

Areas: feet/calves → quads/hips → chest/pecs.
Tools: ball, roller, or hands.
Rule: "Better after than before." Stop if pain spikes.
Why: Hydrated fascia = more flow, less "stickiness" around emotions.

4. Psoas Unwind (Hip Flexor + Diaphragm Pair, 4 minutes)

Diaphragm release: 1 hand low ribs, slow exhale, melt ribs down × 5.

- **Supported lunge stretch:** 90–120s each side, glute engaged, ribs stacked.
  Result: Less fight–flight, more grounded receiving.

5. Jaw–Tongue–Throat Release (3 minutes)

- Tip of tongue to roof (behind teeth), slow exhale "ssss."
- Gentle knuckle massage to masseter/temples.
- Big yawn stretch; sigh out.
  Why: Unspoken words live here; vocal channel frees action.

6. Posture Anchors (30-second micro-resets)

- **Wall stack:** heels, sacrum, ribs, skull to wall; tiny chin tuck; breathe × 5.
- **Desk 1–1–1:** every hour: 1 minute stand, 1 shoulder roll set, 1 chest open.
  Small, often > long, seldom.

7. Shake & Stomp (1–2 minutes)

Bounce, let limbs jiggle, then 20 firm stomps.
Why: Completes stress cycles; tells body "threat passed."

8. Circulation Sprint (3 minutes)

10 air squats → 10 wall pushups → 30s brisk walk (repeat).
Why: Flushes chemistry, lifts mood, returns focus.

9. Heat + Stretch + Breath (Evening Trifecta, 10 minutes)

Warm shower, chest/hip openers, 6–7 count exhales.
Why: Down-regulates for deep sleep (ultimate repair).

10. Nervous System Budgeting

Pick 1: **sleep**, **movement**, or **nutrition** to up-level for 7 days.

- Sleep: fixed wake time + phone out of bedroom.
- Movement: 20-minute walk daily.
- Nutrition: protein + fiber at breakfast; hydrate 2–3 L/day.
  Why: Capacity is biology, not just mindset.

11. Boundaries in the Body

Notice where you collapse/overextend. Practice **"No" with posture**: feet grounded, ribs stacked, soft jaw, coherent breath. Your spine *is* a boundary.

12. Receiving Practice (Somatic)

Lie down; place one hand on heart, one on low belly. 10 coherent breaths while imagining being seen/paid/cherished. Track where tension argues—then exhale from that spot. Trains the body that receiving is **safe**.

13. Environment Upgrades (reduce physiological load)

- Light: morning daylight 5–10 min; dim lights 1 hr pre-bed.
- Sound: white noise to cut micro-startles.

- Ergonomics: screen at eye level, hips above knees, feet supported.
- Air/Temp: fresh air breaks; slightly cooler bedroom.

14. Somatic Scheduling (Capacity-first calendar)

Anchor **movement, meals, breath, sleep** in the calendar *before* high-stakes work. What gets scheduled, stabilizes.

15. Professional Bodywork (as needed)

PT, chiro, massage, myofascial release, pelvic floor, acupuncture—pick support that matches your pattern. Pair sessions with breath/home care so changes hold.

Quick Identify–Clear Flow (4 Minutes)

1. **Name the hotspot:** jaw / ribs / hips.
2. **Score tension:** 0–10.
3. **Do one tool:** coherent breath + targeted release for that zone.
4. **Re-score:** aim for a 1–3 point drop.
5. **One proof step:** a tiny aligned action right after (send the email, finish the invoice, book the call). *Capacity →action → capacity* seals the change.

Prompts & Scripts

- "My body says **no** when I ____. My aligned yes feels like ____."
- "The place I hold stress most is ____. I will tend it at **(time)** daily."
- "If success felt physically safe, my breath/posture would be ____."

Mantras:

- *My body is a partner, not a problem.*
- *More ease, more staying power.*
- *I build capacity faster than I add load.*

Common Pitfalls (and Fixes)

- **All-or-nothing workouts → flare-ups**
  - ○ *Fix:* micro-doses (5–10 minutes) daily; consistency over intensity.
- **Skipping sleep to "hustle"**
  - ○ *Fix:* protect wake time; treat evening like a landing strip.
- **Only mindset, no body care**
  - ○ *Fix:* pair every cognitive reframe with a 60–90s somatic reset.
- **Chronic sitting**
  - ○ *Fix:* 1–1–1 rule each hour (stand 1 min, mobilize 1 area, breathe 1 min).

How You'll Know It's Working

- Less pain/tension; easier, deeper breaths.
- Stable energy across the day; fewer crashes.
- Sleep improves; you wake restored.
- After wins, you *don't* collapse—you integrate and keep going.
- Manifestations stick—and compound.

One-Page Worksheet (for your workbook)

- Loudest body zone today: _____
- Tension score (0–10): _____
- Trigger I suspect: _____

- Tool I'll use (pick 1–2):
  _____

- New score after 3–5 minutes: _____
- One aligned action I'll take now:
  _____

- Capacity habit for 7 days (sleep/move/nourish):
  _____

Bottom Line:
Lasting manifestation requires a body that can hold it. When you clear physical blocks and build capacity, success stops feeling like a sprint and starts feeling like your *new normal.*

What To Do When It Is "Conflict" Blocks

Manifestation doesn't happen in isolation—you live in a web of relationships, communities, and collective realities. Sometimes, your desires run smoothly in that web. Other times, they **collide** with someone else's. When two or more manifestations clash, resistance builds. This doesn't mean your dream is impossible—it means you've hit a **conflict block**.

Conflict blocks aren't proof you're "bad at manifesting." They're reminders that your energy interacts with others' energy. If you don't clear or navigate the conflict, the result can feel unstable, delayed, or sabotaged.

COMMON SIGNS OF CONFLICT BLOCKS

- **Relationship Tension:** You want harmony, but a partner, family member, or friend unconsciously fuels drama.
- **Workplace Friction:** You manifest the job, but the company culture resists your vision.
- **Money Conflicts:** You call in abundance, but joint finances, business partners, or collaborators drain or redirect it.
- **Group Manifestations:** In families, teams, or partnerships, mixed intentions dilute the energy. (One wants expansion, another wants safety.)
- **Push–Pull Energy:** You feel momentum, but every step forward meets external pushback—like invisible brakes.

WHY CONFLICT BLOCKS MAKE SUCCESS SLIP

Manifestations are fragile when built on tangled energy. If your desire rests on another person's unwillingness, fear, or opposing manifestation, it can destabilize. Often, what "falls apart" isn't the manifestation itself—it's the **entanglement** holding it.

Example:

- You manifest the "perfect" relationship, but your partner isn't aligned in their healing—so the connection fractures.
- You manifest a business deal, but the other party values short-term profit while you value long-term integrity—so the deal unravels.
- You manifest peace in your home, but a roommate thrives on chaos—so your nervous system stays on edge.

Conflict blocks show you where you need to untangle, renegotiate, or reset energy.

WAYS TO IDENTIFY CONFLICT BLOCKS
1. Pattern Check

- Do setbacks only happen around certain people?
- Does progress collapse when you involve specific groups?

2. Language Audit

Listen for phrases like:

- "I don't want this."
- "That's not realistic."
- "We can't afford that."

- "What if it fails?"
  These reveal competing intentions.

3. Emotional Scan

Notice how you feel in others' presence. If your body contracts (tight chest, shallow breath, jaw tension) whenever you discuss your dream, you're in an energy clash.

4. Dream Clash Journal

Write your manifestation on one side of a page. On the other, write what you sense the other person wants. Compare. Where they diverge = the block.

5. Collective Conditioning Check

Ask: "Is this resistance truly *theirs*—or a shared belief we both inherited from family, culture, or society?"

WAYS TO CLEAR CONFLICT BLOCKS AT THE ROOT

1. Clarify Your Own Desire

Before engaging others, make sure your desire is crystal clear. Conflict grows when your energy wavers.

- Write your manifestation in "I" language (not "we" or "they").
- Anchor it in your body with breath, hand on heart, affirmation.

2. Detangle Energetic Cords

- Visualize cords connecting you and the other person.
- Gently pull them out at the root, hand them back with compassion.

- Say: "I return your energy to you, and I reclaim mine." This resets the relationship without cutting ties.

3. Dialogue with Compassion

Conflict often hides unspoken fears. Invite conversation.

- "Here's what I'm creating…"
- "What feels supportive to you in this?"
- "Where do our visions overlap?"
  True alignment sometimes requires renegotiation, not force.

4. Create "Energetic Boundaries"

- Visualize a golden bubble around your field.
- Say: "I allow my manifestations to flow without interference."
- Meet others from this shielded state.

5. Neutralize Their Fear

If others' resistance stems from fear, you can stabilize the energy:

- **Silent practice:** When they express doubt, breathe and silently affirm: "I choose alignment. Their fear is not mine."
- **Spoken practice:** "I hear your concern. I appreciate it. And I trust this path."

6. Shift from Entanglement to Parallel Play

Instead of fighting over one "shared outcome," allow both realities to exist.

- "I choose expansion."
- "They choose safety."
  Both can coexist if you honor sovereignty.

7. Collective Reframe

If family or team patterns are strong, create a reframe:

- "My success doesn't take from them."
- "There is space for both."
- "I thrive, they thrive."

8. Ritual for Clearing Conflict

- Write their name + fear/doubt on paper.
- Burn, bury, or dissolve it in water, saying: "I release entanglement. I honor their path and walk mine."

Prompts & Scripts

- "Where am I carrying someone else's fears as my own?"
- "What part of this conflict belongs to me, and what part belongs to them?"
- "How can I honor both paths without abandoning mine?"

Mantras:

- *I untangle with compassion.*
- *Their fears are not my destiny.*
- *Alignment dissolves resistance.*

Common Pitfalls (and Fixes)

- **Trying to manifest *for* someone else**
  - *Fix:* Return to your lane. Anchor your desire in "I" statements.

- **Forcing agreement before alignment**
  - *Fix:* Allow time. Trust clarity over control.
- **Over-giving to keep peace**
  - *Fix:* Ask: "Does this compromise collapse me or sustain me?"
- **Confusing rejection with failure**
  - *Fix:* Reframe: "Their no redirects me to a clearer yes."

How You'll Know It's Working

- Conversations feel lighter, not combative.
- Your body feels safe to share desires.
- You no longer dim or delay your dreams to "keep the peace."
- Success flows even if others remain skeptical.
- Relationships become cleaner—supportive or clearly separate.

Conflict blocks don't mean your manifestation is doomed. They are invitations to disentangle from others' energy, strengthen your own foundation, and navigate relationships with clarity and compassion. When you clear conflict at the root, you stop leaking energy—and your manifestations finally have room to last.

What To Do When It Is An "Energetic" Block

Not all blocks live in the mind or emotions. Some are **energetic**—subtle yet powerful disruptions in your field that stop manifestation from flowing smoothly. You might feel mentally clear and emotionally balanced, yet still notice your desires stalling, collapsing, or slipping away. This is often a sign that your energy is tangled, stagnant, or out of alignment.

Energetic blocks can come from many sources:

- Carrying the weight of other people's expectations or emotions.
- Holding onto old experiences as "imprints" in the body.
- Running on command-and-demand energy without grounding it in reflection.
- Leaks or entanglements in relationships, workplaces, or even ancestral patterns.

When energy is blocked, it's like trying to pour water through a clogged pipe—no matter how strong your intention, flow is restricted. Healing at the energetic root means clearing the channel so life-force can move freely again.

The good news is, energy responds quickly to awareness and intention. Through practices like grounding, breathwork, visualization, sound, movement, and clearing rituals, you can release stagnant energy, dissolve entanglements, and restore alignment. When you do, manifestation feels less like forcing and more like *flowing*.

In the pages that follow, we'll explore practical ways to identify and release energetic blocks so you can hold your power with steadiness, clarity, and ease.

Key Insight

Energetic blocks aren't about "bad vibes." They are simply **places where flow has been interrupted or entangled.** Healing at the root means clearing, grounding, and protecting your field so your energy matches your desire. When energy is clear, manifestation doesn't have to be forced—it flows.

1. Energy Awareness Scan

Just as you might notice tension in your shoulders or a knot in your stomach, your energy body also holds signals of stress, stagnation, or flow. These subtle cues often show up before physical symptoms or emotional spirals, yet most people overlook them.

An **Energy Awareness Scan** teaches you to listen inwardly, mapping where your life force feels open and where it feels stuck. This simple daily practice becomes the foundation of energetic hygiene—like brushing your teeth, but for your aura and alignment.

HOW TO PRACTICE
Step 1 – Settle Into Stillness

- Sit or lie down comfortably.
- Close your eyes and take 3–5 slow breaths, releasing tension on the exhale.

Step 2 – Begin the Scan

- Start at the top of your head and slowly move your awareness downward.
- Move through each area: head → neck → chest → stomach → hips → legs → feet.

Step 3 – Notice Sensations

- Ask gently: *"What do I feel here?"*
- Common cues: heaviness, tingling, warmth, pressure, or numbness.
- There is no wrong answer—just notice.

Step 4 – Label With Simplicity

- Say silently: *"This feels light."* or *"This feels blocked."*
- Don't overanalyze—just identify the quality.

Step 5 – Pause Where It Feels Heavy

- If an area feels blocked, breathe into it.
- Imagine sending gentle attention and light there, as if opening a window in a stuffy room.

Step 6 – Complete the Scan

- Once you reach your feet, take a full breath and imagine your whole body surrounded by light.
- Whisper: *"I am aware. I am aligned. I am open."*

Example Awareness Notes

- "Chest feels tight, like a weight."
- "Stomach feels numb—hard to connect there."
- "Hands feel tingly, open."

Journaling Prompt

- *"Where in my body feels most open today?"*
- *"Where do I notice heaviness or numbness?"*
- *"If this block had a message, it might be…"*

Why This Works

Energy blocks thrive in unconsciousness. By simply noticing where you feel heavy or light, you shift from autopilot to awareness. This awareness alone begins to soften resistance, making the block ready for deeper clearing practices.

2. Breathwork for Clearing

Breath is the bridge between body, mind, and energy. When energy feels stuck, shallow, or erratic breathing often reflects it. By consciously adjusting your breath, you can shift your nervous system, release stagnant energy, and recharge your body with fresh life force.

Breathwork doesn't have to be complex. Even a few intentional minutes of long exhales and visualization can transform how you feel—clearing what's heavy and making space for lightness.

HOW TO PRACTICE
Step 1 – Position

- Sit comfortably with your spine upright, or lie flat if preferred.
- Rest one hand on your belly, the other on your chest.

Step 2 – Set Intention

- Whisper to yourself: *"I breathe out what no longer serves me. I breathe in light and renewal."*

Step 3 – Establish the Rhythm

- Inhale through your nose for **4 counts**.
- Exhale gently through your mouth for **8 counts**.
- Continue for at least 6–10 cycles.

Step 4 – Add Visualization

- On each inhale, imagine golden light filling your body.
- On each exhale, picture stagnant energy leaving as dark smoke, mist, or heaviness dissolving.
- See the light growing brighter with every cycle.

Step 5 – Close With Integration

- After a few minutes, return to normal breathing.
- Place both hands over your heart and say: *"I am clear. I am open. I am aligned."*

Optional Variations

- **Box Breath (4–4–4–4):** balances energy when you feel scattered.
- **Breath of Fire (rapid exhales):** energizes when you feel heavy or stuck.
- **Sighing Exhale:** long, audible sighs to release tension instantly.

Journaling Prompt

- *"When I exhaled, I released…"*
- *"The light I inhaled felt like…"*
- *"After this breathwork, I feel…"*

Why This Works

The nervous system and energy field mirror one another. Long exhales activate the parasympathetic system (calm, release), while visualization programs the subconscious to clear what's stuck. Breathwork not only moves air but also moves energy, transforming blocks into flow.

3. Grounding Into the Earth

When energy feels chaotic—too much input, racing thoughts, or anxiety—the body loses its sense of stability. Grounding reconnects you with the earth's steady frequency, clearing excess energy and restoring balance.

Think of grounding as plugging yourself into the planet's natural rhythm. The earth absorbs heaviness you no longer need and replenishes you with calm strength.

HOW TO PRACTICE
Step 1 – Find Your Ground

- Stand barefoot on grass, soil, or floor (outdoors is best, but indoors works too).
- Keep your feet hip-width apart, knees soft, shoulders relaxed.

Step 2 – Breathe Into Presence

- Inhale through your nose, exhale slowly through your mouth.
- Feel your body weight sinking gently into your feet.

Step 3 – Visualize Roots

- Imagine roots extending from the soles of your feet deep into the earth.
- See them anchoring you into soil, rock, and core layers below.

Step 4 – Release Downward

- With each exhale, send heavy, stagnant, or anxious energy down through the roots.

- Visualize it dissolving into the earth, where it can be recycled.

Step 5 – Receive Upward

- With each inhale, draw nourishing, light energy upward through your roots.
- See it rising into your legs, belly, chest, and heart.
- Feel calm, stability, and strength filling your whole body.

Step 6 – Close the Practice

- Place your hands on your heart.
- Whisper: *"I am grounded. I am steady. I am supported."*

Optional Variations

- **Seated version:** Sit in a chair with both feet flat on the ground.
- **Walking version:** Walk slowly barefoot, imagining roots with each step.
- **Crystal support:** Hold or place grounding stones (hematite, smoky quartz, obsidian) as anchors.

Journaling Prompt

- *"The energy I released into the earth was…"*
- *"The energy I received back felt like…"*
- *"Grounding helped me feel more…"*

Why This Works

Anxiety and overstimulation often come from living in the head and disconnecting from the body. Grounding anchors awareness downward, balancing scattered energy with the earth's stability.

4. Movement & Shaking

Energy isn't just stored in the mind—it lives in the body. When emotions or stress aren't expressed, they often lodge in the muscles and tissues, creating tension or heaviness. Movement and shaking are some of the fastest ways to release that stored energy.

Animals do this naturally—after stress, they shake to reset their nervous systems. Humans have forgotten this instinct, but we can reclaim it. Just a minute or two of shaking or free movement can reset your body, clear stagnant energy, and restore flow.

HOW TO PRACTICE
Step 1 – Set the Space

- Stand with feet hip-width apart.
- Loosen your arms and legs, letting them feel relaxed.

Step 2 – Begin Shaking

- Start with your hands, then arms, shoulders, torso, hips, legs, and feet.
- Shake each area for a few seconds, then shake your whole body together.

Step 3 – Add Rhythm or Sound (Optional)

- Play music and let your body move with it.
- Stomp your feet into the ground to release heaviness.
- Add sighs, hums, or laughter if it feels natural.

Step 4 – Let It Be Intuitive

- Allow your body to move however it wants—big, small, silly, or wild.

- There is no "wrong" way to move. The goal is release, not performance.

Step 5 – Close With Stillness

- After 1–2 minutes, pause.
- Stand or sit quietly, noticing tingling, warmth, or lightness.
- Whisper: *"I am clear. I am free. I am reset."*

Optional Variations

- **Micro-shakes:** Shake your hands and arms under your desk for 30 seconds if you're in public.
- **Dance release:** Put on one song and let your body move however it wants.
- **Stomp grounding:** Stomp your feet firmly, imagining old energy leaving through the soles.

Journaling Prompt

- *"The energy I shook loose felt like…"*
- *"After moving, my body feels…"*
- *"This practice showed me I can release energy by…"*

Why This Works

Movement and shaking discharge stress from the nervous system and prevent stuck energy from hardening into long-term tension. By letting your body express itself freely, you restore natural flow and make space for fresh energy to enter.

5. Sound & Vibration

Sound is energy made audible. Every vibration you create or receive ripples through your body, influencing your cells, nervous system, and energy field. When energy feels dense or blocked, sound acts like a tuning fork for your system—it shakes loose heaviness and restores harmony.

You don't need to be a singer or musician. Your own voice, a simple hum, or even a single tone can move more energy than silence ever could. And when paired with tools like bowls, forks, or drums, the effect deepens.

HOW TO PRACTICE
Practice 1 – Humming for Clearing

- Sit comfortably, close your eyes.
- Inhale deeply, then hum on the exhale.
- Focus the vibration into areas of heaviness (chest, throat, head).
- Continue for 5–10 breaths.

Best for: anxiety, blocked throat chakra, scattered energy.

Practice 2 – Toning / Chanting

- Choose a sound such as **"OM"**, **"AH"**, or a vowel (A, E, I, O, U).
- Inhale, then sustain the tone on the exhale.
- Let the vibration fill your body and radiate outward.
- Repeat for 2–3 minutes.

Best for: grounding, aligning energy, calming overthinking.

Practice 3 – Sound Tools

- **Singing Bowls:** Strike or circle the rim to create continuous tones that wash through your field.
- **Tuning Forks:** Strike and place near energy centers or over areas of heaviness.
- **Drumming:** Steady rhythm grounds and clears dense or stagnant energy.
- **Chimes or Bells:** Short bursts of high-frequency sound that "cut through" stuckness.

Best for: deep clearing, meditation, or group energy work.

Practice 4 – Directed Vibration

- Place your hands on the area of your body that feels blocked.
- Hum, chant, or tone into that spot.
- Imagine the vibration dissolving heaviness and restoring flow.

Journaling Prompt

- *"The sound that cleared me most today was…"*
- *"When I let vibration move through me, I felt…"*
- *"The message in the sound was…"*

Why This Works

Blocked energy often creates contraction or stagnation. Sound introduces movement, resonance, and flow. The body and energy field naturally harmonize to vibration, which is why sound has been used in healing traditions for thousands of years.

6. *Visualization of Flow*

Energy thrives on movement. When it stagnates, you feel heavy, tired, or blocked. Visualization is a simple way to restore flow by using the imagination as a guide for the body's subtle energy.

Your subconscious responds powerfully to imagery. When you picture light, water, or movement flowing through you, your energy field often mirrors that picture—softening, releasing, and clearing on its own.

HOW TO PRACTICE
Step 1 – Get Comfortable

- Sit or lie down with eyes closed.
- Take 3 slow breaths, relaxing your shoulders and jaw.

Step 2 – Call In the Flow

- Imagine a **river of light** (golden, silver, or any color that feels healing) entering the crown of your head.
- See or sense it moving slowly through your entire body.

Step 3 – Notice the Blocks

- As the light or river flows, notice where it slows, pools, or feels stuck.
- Example: heavy in the chest, thick in the stomach, numb in the legs.

Step 4 – Breathe Into the Spot

- Focus on that area.
- Inhale gently into it, expanding space.
- Exhale and imagine the light washing away heaviness.
- Continue until the flow feels smoother.

Step 5 – Complete the Cycle

- See the river exiting through your feet, flowing deep into the earth.
- Imagine the earth recycling what you released into nourishment and balance.

Optional Variations

- **Shower Visualization:** Imagine standing under golden water that rinses energy away.
- **Wind Visualization:** Picture a breeze moving through your body, sweeping out stagnation.
- **Fire Visualization:** Envision warmth burning away heaviness and leaving clarity.

Journaling Prompt

- *"The part of my body where energy slowed was…"*
- *"When I breathed into it, I felt…"*
- *"Now my flow feels more like…"*

Why This Works

Energy follows awareness. When you picture flow, you direct your body's subtle systems to mimic that image. The mind relaxes, the nervous system resets, and energy naturally clears.

7. Cord Release / Energetic Detachment

Every interaction—whether loving, stressful, or unresolved—creates an energetic cord. These cords connect you to people, places, or even old experiences. Some cords nourish you, but others drain your energy, keeping you tied to resentment, guilt, or unfinished stories.

Cord release isn't about rejecting others or erasing the past. It's about lovingly detaching from what no longer serves you, reclaiming your power, and sealing your field so you stay clear.

HOW TO PRACTICE
Step 1 – Prepare the Space

- Sit quietly, close your eyes, and place a hand on your heart.
- Take 3 deep breaths, grounding yourself in calm awareness.

Step 2 – Visualize the Cords

- Imagine cords of energy extending from your body to others.
- They may appear as threads, ropes, beams of light, or even colors.
- Notice where they attach (heart, solar plexus, throat, etc.).

Step 3 – Identify One to Release

- Focus on a cord that feels heavy, draining, or no longer aligned.
- Silently say: *"I honor this connection, and I now release it with love."*

Step 4 – Gently Remove the Cord

- Visualize yourself pulling the cord out at the root.
- Hand it back to the person or situation with compassion.
- Whisper: *"This is yours to carry, not mine."*

Step 5 – Seal the Space

- See the empty space filled with golden light, love, or gratitude.
- Imagine your whole energy field being sealed and strengthened with light.

Step 6 – Close the Practice

- Place both hands over your heart.
- Say: *"I am whole. I am clear. I am free."*
- Take one grounding breath before opening your eyes.

Optional Variations

- **Writing Cord Release:** Write a letter to the person or situation, then safely burn or tear it.
- **Physical Gesture:** Sweep your hands gently around your body to symbolically "clear cords."
- **Night Ritual:** Use before bed to release the day's interactions.

Journaling Prompt

- *"The cord I released today was tied to…"*
- *"After the release, I felt…"*
- *"The light I replaced it with was…"*

Why This Works

Unwanted cords act like energetic leaks, draining your clarity and power. By consciously releasing them and filling the space with love, you prevent new negative attachments from forming.

8. Aura Brushing / Smudging

Your aura—the energy field surrounding your body—acts like a sponge. It absorbs impressions, emotions, and energies from people and environments you encounter. Over time, this buildup can feel heavy, foggy, or "not yours."

Aura brushing and smudging are simple ways to clear this layer, restoring clarity and lightness. Think of it as brushing dust off your energy body so your natural radiance can shine again.

HOW TO PRACTICE AURA BRUSHING

Step 1 – Get Present

- Stand or sit comfortably.
- Take 3 slow breaths, centering yourself.

Step 2 – Sweep the Field

- Extend your hands a few inches away from your body.
- Starting from the top of your head, sweep downward slowly, as if brushing off dust.
- Move down the front, sides, and back of your body.
- With each sweep, imagine heaviness falling away.

Step 3 – Release

- Shake your hands out after each sweep as if flicking off old energy.
- Whisper: *"This is not mine. I release it."*

Step 4 – Seal the Aura

- When finished, imagine a layer of golden or white light surrounding your body.
- Say: *"I am clear. I am safe. I am in my own energy."*

Optional Smudging Tools

- **Sage or Palo Santo:** Burn safely and waft smoke gently around your body.
- **Incense:** Hold in one hand, trace the smoke around your field.
- **Essential Oils:** Place a drop in your palms, rub together, and sweep the scent around your aura.
- **Sound:** Bells or chimes can also "smudge" the aura vibrationally.

Journaling Prompt

- *"After brushing my aura, I felt…"*
- *"What I released today was…"*
- *"My energy feels lighter because…"*

Why This Works

Just as your body needs a shower, your aura needs regular clearing. Brushing or smudging removes stagnant or external energies so you can return to alignment. When your field is clear, you feel lighter, calmer, and more connected to your own power.

9. Water as a Cleanser

Water is nature's universal purifier. Just as it washes dirt from the body, it can also cleanse stagnant energy, emotions, and heaviness from your field. Across cultures and traditions, water has been used for renewal—baptisms, river immersions, sacred baths, and ocean rituals.

When you intentionally use water as a cleanser, it becomes more than hygiene—it becomes an energetic reset.

HOW TO PRACTICE
Practice 1 – Shower Ritual

1. Step into the shower and take three grounding breaths.
2. As the water flows, imagine it carrying away old energy, stress, or heaviness.
3. Visualize the water turning gray or dark as it leaves, then clearing as it hits the drain.
4. End by picturing fresh golden or white light pouring over you with the water.
5. Whisper: *"I am washed clear. I am renewed."*

Practice 2 – Bath with Salt or Herbs

1. Fill a tub with warm water.
2. Add sea salt, Epsom salt, or herbs (lavender, rosemary, chamomile).
3. Soak for 15–20 minutes, allowing heaviness to dissolve.
4. As you drain the tub, imagine all stuck energy leaving your body with the water.

Best for: deep emotional clearing, heaviness in the body, or after intense interactions.

Practice 3 – Natural Water Reset

1. Visit a lake, river, or the ocean if possible.
2. Step into the water, even if only with your feet or hands.
3. Ask the water to cleanse and reset your field.
4. Stand, float, or submerge while imagining the natural current restoring balance.

Best for: feeling disconnected, anxious, or energetically drained.

Optional Variations

- **Water Bowl Ritual:** Dip your hands into a bowl of water, wash your face or arms intentionally.
- **Drinking Water with Intention:** Whisper a blessing (*"This water cleanses me"*) before drinking.
- **Rain Ritual:** Stand in the rain briefly, imagining each drop clearing you.

Journaling Prompt

- *"The energy I released into the water was…"*
- *"After cleansing, I felt…"*
- *"Water teaches me that release can be…"*

Why This Works

Water conducts energy, absorbs heaviness, and restores flow. Whether through a simple shower or the vastness of the ocean, it offers an instant energetic reset. When you use water intentionally, it not only clears blocks but also reconnects you to nature's rhythm of renewal.

10. Gratitude Anchoring

Entitlement and energetic heaviness dissolve in gratitude. When you focus only on what you don't have, your energy contracts, creating scarcity and resentment. Gratitude expands your field, stabilizes your vibration, and reminds you that abundance is already present.

Gratitude isn't just about manners—it's an energetic practice. By consistently anchoring into appreciation, you align yourself with the frequency of abundance. This makes it easier to hold onto manifestations without slipping into arrogance, jealousy, or emptiness.

HOW TO PRACTICE
Step 1 – Daily Gratitude Ritual

- Each day, speak or write down 3 specific things you're grateful for.
- Go beyond vague answers—detail anchors the feeling.
    - *"I'm grateful for the warmth of sunlight on my face this morning."*
    - *"I'm grateful for the friend who sent me an encouraging text."*
    - *"I'm grateful for my persistence in writing one page today."*

Step 2 – Gratitude for Flow

- Include gratitude for what's already moving smoothly in your life.
- Example: *"I'm grateful that my creativity flows when I journal."*
- Recognizing ease reinforces it, strengthening the channels of abundance.

Step 3 – Gratitude in Challenge

- When stuck in heaviness, pause and name one thing you can still appreciate.
- Example: *"Even though I feel uncertain, I'm grateful I have tools to shift this."*
- Gratitude doesn't erase challenge, but it prevents blocks from taking over your entire field.

Step 4 – Embody the Energy

- Place a hand on your heart as you say each gratitude.
- Breathe deeply and let the emotion of appreciation spread through your chest and body.
- This shifts gratitude from a thought into a felt vibration.

Journaling Prompts

- *"Right now, I'm most grateful for…"*
- *"One area of life that flows easily is…"*
- *"Even in challenge, I can appreciate…"*

Why This Works

Gratitude is the opposite of entitlement. Where entitlement says *"I'm owed,"* gratitude says *"I'm blessed."* By practicing gratitude daily, you stabilize your energy, dissolve resentment, and create resonance with abundance. Manifestations not only arrive more easily—they stay, because your field matches their frequency.

11. Energy Boundaries

Your energy field is porous—it naturally interacts with the people and environments around you. While this can create connection, it also means you may absorb energy that isn't yours: stress, resentment, even other people's desires. Without boundaries, your manifestations get tangled with external influences.

Energy boundaries don't close you off from life. They create a clear container: what's yours stays steady, and what isn't yours flows out. This keeps you aligned with your own path, not pulled into someone else's.

HOW TO PRACTICE
Step 1 – Visualize Your Boundary

- Close your eyes and imagine a golden bubble, shield, or aura of light surrounding your body.
- See it about an arm's length away, fully enclosing you in a sphere of safety.

Step 2 – Set the Intention

Say clearly, out loud or silently:

- *"I keep what's mine. I release what's not."*
- *"Only love and alignment may enter."*

Step 3 – Strengthen With Breath

- Inhale: imagine your bubble filling with golden light.
- Exhale: see any heaviness, cords, or foreign energy dissolving outside of it.

Step 4 – Reapply as Needed

- Use this practice daily in the morning, before entering crowds, or after draining conversations.
- Re-visualize your boundary anytime you feel "invaded" or overwhelmed.

Optional Variations

- **Mirror Shield:** Imagine your bubble as mirrored on the outside, reflecting negativity away.
- **Elemental Shield:** Picture your bubble made of fire, water, earth, or air depending on what feels strong.
- **Crystals:** Carry stones like black tourmaline or obsidian to reinforce the field.

Journaling Prompt

- *"When I strengthen my boundaries, I notice…"*
- *"The energy I most often absorb from others is…"*
- *"The boundary I choose to reinforce daily is…"*

Why This Works

Manifestation thrives in clarity. Without boundaries, your field carries clutter that isn't yours, confusing your focus and draining your energy. By setting strong energetic boundaries, you protect your power, honor your alignment, and create space for your manifestations to root firmly.

12. Elemental Balancing

When energy feels blocked, often one of the four classical elements—Fire, Earth, Water, or Air—is out of harmony. Each element carries a distinct quality that supports the flow of life force. By intentionally working with them, you can restore balance and dissolve stagnation at the root.

THE FOUR ELEMENTS IN PRACTICE
Fire – Inspiration & Clarity

- **Qualities:** passion, motivation, illumination.
- **When out of balance:** you feel drained, uninspired, or unclear about direction.
- **Practices:**
    - Light a candle and meditate on its flame.
    - Spend time in sunlight, absorbing warmth and vitality.
    - Write intentions by candlelight to ignite clarity.

Earth – Stability & Support

- **Qualities:** grounding, structure, nourishment.
- **When out of balance:** you feel anxious, scattered, or insecure.
- **Practices:**
    - Walk barefoot on grass or soil.
    - Place grounding crystals (hematite, smoky quartz, jasper) in your space.

o Surround yourself with plants or touch the earth with your hands.

Water – Flow & Renewal

- **Qualities:** emotional release, intuition, cleansing.
- **When out of balance:** you feel stuck in emotions, heavy, or rigid.
- **Practices:**
    o Take a salt bath or shower with cleansing intention.
    o Swim or wade in rivers, lakes, or oceans.
    o Drink water slowly, imagining it hydrating your energy as well as your body.

Air – Mental Clarity & Breath

- **Qualities:** communication, perspective, spaciousness.
- **When out of balance:** you feel mentally cluttered, overthinking, or restless.
- **Practices:**
    o Do breathwork (inhale 4, exhale 8).
    o Spend time outdoors in the wind or fresh air.
    o Open windows to circulate stagnant energy in your environment.

HOW TO USE ELEMENTAL BALANCING

1. **Identify the Imbalance**
    o Ask: *"Do I feel uninspired, unstable, heavy, or mentally cluttered?"*
    o This points to which element needs attention.
2. **Choose One Practice**
    o Pick a simple ritual with that element (light a candle, walk barefoot, take a bath, breathe outdoors).
3. **Anchor the Shift**

- As you engage with the element, set an intention:
  - Fire: *"I ignite my clarity."*
  - Earth: *"I ground into stability."*
  - Water: *"I allow flow and release."*
  - Air: *"I clear my mind and expand my perspective."*

Journaling Prompt

- *"The element I feel most disconnected from is..."*
- *"A practice I can do today to rebalance is..."*
- *"After this practice, I felt..."*

Why This Works

The elements are timeless forces of nature that mirror your inner world. By reconnecting with Fire, Earth, Water, and Air, you bring your energy field back into harmony. Balanced elements create flow, stability, and clarity—fertile ground for manifestation to take root.

13. Releasing Through the Voice

The voice is one of the most powerful—and underused—tools for clearing energy. When emotions or blocks get stuck in the throat or chest, they often show up as tightness, heaviness, or difficulty expressing yourself. Using your voice intentionally—through sighs, groans, chants, or even roars—creates vibration that shakes loose what words alone cannot.

You don't have to be a singer. Your voice is an instrument of release and alignment, always available to you.

HOW TO PRACTICE
Step 1 – Create Space

- Find a private space where you feel safe to make sounds without holding back.
- Stand or sit upright, shoulders relaxed, jaw loose.

Step 2 – Choose Your Release Style

- **Sighing:** Take a deep inhale and let out a long, exaggerated sigh. Repeat 3–5 times.
- **Groaning:** Hum or groan low in your chest, letting the vibration soften tension.
- **Chanting:** Repeat a simple sound like *"OM"* or *"AH"* to harmonize energy.
- **Roaring:** Inhale deeply, then exhale with a strong roar (into a pillow if needed).

Step 3 – Direct the Sound

- Focus on the area that feels blocked (throat, chest, or heart).
- Imagine the sound waves vibrating and dissolving the heaviness.

Step 4 – Close With Calm

- Place a hand on your chest or throat.
- Breathe deeply and whisper: *"I am open. I am free. My voice carries truth."*

Optional Variations

- **Voice Journaling:** Speak aloud everything you feel without censoring, then end with a clearing sigh.
- **Sound & Movement Combo:** Shake your body while groaning or sighing for deeper release.

- **Sacred Chanting:** Use mantras or prayer sounds if aligned with your spiritual practice.

Journaling Prompt

- *"When I released through my voice, I felt…"*
- *"The sound that cleared me most was…"*
- *"My throat and chest now feel…"*

Why This Works

Blocks often silence the voice, keeping truth and emotion suppressed. Sound vibrates through tissue and energy fields, shaking loose what words can't express. By releasing through your voice, you reclaim expression, open flow in the throat and chest, and strengthen your alignment with authentic power.

14. Reiki, Energy Healing, or Self-Hand Placement

Your hands are natural conduits of energy. Whether you practice Reiki, other healing modalities, or simply tune into your own inner light, placing your hands with intention can restore balance where it is needed most. The warmth, pressure, and flow of energy provide comfort and signal to your body and spirit that healing is present.

Self-hand placement is one of the simplest yet most powerful ways to shift blocked energy. You don't need any formal training—just the willingness to trust that energy follows focus, and your touch can become a channel of restoration.

HOW TO PRACTICE

Step 1 – Center Yourself
• Sit or lie in a quiet space where you can relax.
• Close your eyes and take 3–5 deep, slow breaths.
• Imagine your body surrounded by gentle light.

Step 2 – Scan for Energy Blocks
• Ask yourself: *"Where in my body feels heavy, tight, or out of balance?"*
• Common areas include the heart (emotional pain), the gut (intuition and anxiety), or the head (mental overwhelm).

Step 3 – Place Your Hands
• Gently place one or both hands on the area that feels blocked.
• If unsure, rest your hands over your heart or abdomen—these are natural centers of energy flow.

Step 4 – Direct the Energy
• Visualize warm golden or white light flowing from your palms into the area.
• Imagine the block dissolving, replaced by harmony and ease.
• Whisper or think the affirmation: *"I restore balance here."*

Step 5 – Close With Gratitude
• Slowly remove your hands and rest them on your lap.
• Thank your body and spirit for receiving healing.
• Take a final grounding breath before moving on with your day.

Optional Variations
• **Full-Body Sequence:** Place hands gently on different areas in order—head, throat, heart, stomach, hips, knees, feet—for a complete self-healing session.
• **Crystal Support:** Hold a crystal (such as rose quartz for the heart or amethyst for the mind) under your hand for amplified energy.

• **Distance Intention:** If you feel called, imagine sending healing light to another person, place, or situation.

Journaling Prompt
• "The area that most needed my touch today was…"
• "While my hands rested here, I felt…"
• "Afterward, my energy shifted in the following way…"

Why This Works
Your body naturally responds to touch with relaxation and regulation. Adding intention, visualization, and energy awareness makes that touch profoundly healing. By placing your hands where you feel blocked, you signal both your nervous system and subtle energy field that balance is possible. This simple practice can restore calm, reduce stress, and deepen your connection to your inner wisdom.

15. Crystals & Tools

Crystals have been used for centuries as allies in energy healing, protection, and balance. Each stone carries its own vibration, which can amplify your intentions and support your natural energy field. Tools like crystals are not meant to *do the work for you*—they are conduits, amplifiers, and reminders. When you use them with a clear purpose, they become powerful companions for clearing blocks and restoring harmony.

HOW TO PRACTICE

Step 1 – Choose Your Crystal or Tool
• **Black Tourmaline or Obsidian:** Creates grounding and protective shields, helping you feel safe and anchored.
• **Selenite:** Clears stagnant energy and restores flow, like a gentle energetic broom.
• **Amethyst:** Brings balance, calming the mind and soothing emotional stress.
• Select the one that resonates most with your current need.

Step 2 – Cleanse the Crystal
• Hold under running water, leave in moonlight, or simply breathe onto it with intention.
• Say: *"I clear away all energy that is not mine."*

Step 3 – Program With Intention
• Hold the crystal in both hands, close your eyes, and focus on your desired outcome (protection, balance, clearing).
• Speak or think clearly: *"I charge this stone with the intention of..."* (fill in your words).

Step 4 – Use in Practice
• Place the crystal on or near the area of your body that feels blocked.
• Carry it in your pocket or wear it as jewelry to keep its energy close.
• Place it in your space—on a desk, altar, or nightstand—to create an energetic field of support.

Step 5 – Close the Session
• Thank the crystal for its assistance.
• Return it to a clean, safe place (a pouch, dish, or cloth).

Optional Variations
• **Crystal Grids:** Arrange multiple crystals in geometric patterns to amplify their energy.
• **Crystal + Breathwork:** Hold the crystal in one hand while practicing deep breathing for added focus.
• **Tool Pairing:** Combine crystals with sound tools (like tuning forks or singing bowls) for layered healing.

Journaling Prompt
• "The crystal I was most drawn to today was…"
• "When I held or placed this stone, I noticed…"
• "The shift I experienced with its support was…"

Why This Works
Crystals resonate with specific frequencies, much like tuning forks for your energy field. By combining their vibration with your clear intention, you amplify the effect. This isn't about superstition—it's about focusing your mind, body, and spirit on a desired outcome, with the crystal acting as a physical anchor for that energy.

16. Nature Reset

Nature is one of the most powerful healers. When you step outside, your energy field begins to align with the earth's natural rhythms. Static energy, emotional heaviness, and mental clutter discharge into the ground, while the calming frequencies of trees, water, and fresh air replenish you. Simply being present with nature restores balance without effort—it is the original reset button for your body, mind, and spirit.

How to Practice

Step 1 – Choose Your Setting
• Find a place where you can connect with the natural world: a park, forest, garden, lake, or even your backyard.
• Notice what feels most inviting—trees, grass, water, or sky.

Step 2 – Ground Through the Body
• Sit with your back against a tree and feel its support.
• Walk barefoot on grass, sand, or soil to let energy release through your feet.
• Or lie down on the ground and allow the earth to hold your weight fully.

Step 3 – Breathe With Nature
• Inhale deeply, imagining you are breathing in the life force of the earth.
• Exhale slowly, letting stress and static energy sink into the ground.

• Repeat 5–10 breaths, syncing your rhythm with the natural world.

Step 4 – Open to Renewal
• Notice sounds, smells, textures, and colors around you.
• Imagine your energy field being gently brushed clean and refilled with balance.
• Whisper or affirm: *"I am restored by nature's harmony."*

Step 5 – Close With Gratitude
• Place a hand over your heart and thank the earth for rebalancing you.
• Carry the grounded feeling back into your day.

Optional Variations
• **Water Reset:** Stand in a stream, lake, or ocean and imagine the water washing away stuck energy.
• **Sky Reset:** Lie on your back and gaze at the clouds or stars, letting your mind expand and soften.
• **Micro-Reset:** If you can't go outside, open a window, tend to a houseplant, or place your hands in soil to connect with earth energy.

Journaling Prompt
• "The part of nature I connected with most today was…"
• "While sitting/walking/lying in nature, I felt…"
• "Afterward, my energy field felt…"

Why This Works
The earth carries a natural electromagnetic frequency that aligns with our own. Modern life often disrupts this connection, creating stress and static buildup. Direct contact with nature discharges what doesn't belong and recharges your system with balance. It's a free, accessible, and timeless way to restore your energy field.

17. *Daily Energy Hygiene Ritual*

Just as you brush your teeth and shower to keep your body clean, your energy field also benefits from daily care. Regular practices prevent energetic buildup, stress overload, and emotional burnout. A simple morning and evening ritual keeps your system clear, grounded, and protected—helping you move through the day with resilience and return to rest with ease.

HOW TO PRACTICE

Morning Ritual – Ground + Shield
Step 1 – Ground Yourself
• Stand with feet hip-width apart.
• Imagine roots growing down from your feet into the earth, anchoring you firmly.
• Breathe in through your nose, out through your mouth, releasing any overnight heaviness.

Step 2 – Create a Protective Bubble
• Visualize a sphere of golden or white light surrounding your entire body.
• Say silently or aloud: *"Only energies of love and truth may enter. I am safe and protected."*
• Carry this shield with you throughout the day as your energetic boundary.

Evening Ritual – Shake + Shower Cleanse
Step 1 – Shake It Off
• Stand and gently shake out your arms, legs, shoulders, and torso for 1–2 minutes.
• Imagine all stress and stagnant energy dropping away like dust.

Step 2 – Shower Cleanse
• While showering (or washing your face/hands if no shower), imagine the water rinsing off everything you picked up during

the day.
• Whisper: *"I release what is not mine. I return to balance."*

Optional Variations
• **Salt Bath:** Take an Epsom or sea salt bath once or twice a week for deeper clearing.
• **Smudge or Spray:** Use sage, palo santo, or an energy-clearing spray as part of your evening routine.
• **Micro-Cleanses:** If you feel drained midday, pause to shake your hands vigorously or brush your arms downward to reset.

Journaling Prompt
• "When I grounded and shielded this morning, I felt..."
• "The most noticeable energy I released this evening was..."
• "My body and spirit now feel..."

Why This Works
Energy hygiene is about consistency, not intensity. By grounding and shielding in the morning, you set clear boundaries before the day begins. By shaking and cleansing in the evening, you let go of what isn't yours. Over time, this prevents the slow buildup of stress and energetic debris that can lead to exhaustion or emotional burnout.

Breaking Promises That No Longer Serve

To Self

Step 1 – Name the Promise

First, bring the promise into awareness. Some examples:

- **Inherited Blocks:** "We don't talk about money." (Keeps wealth at bay.)
- **Emotional Blocks:** "I'll never let anyone hurt me again." (Creates walls that also block love.)
- **Mental Blocks:** "I must always be perfect." (Breeds procrastination or burnout.)
- **Physical Blocks:** "I can't slow down or I'll fall behind." (Manifests in exhaustion or chronic tension.)
- **Conflict Blocks:** "I'll always keep the peace." (Prevents honest expression, creates resentment.)
- **Energetic Blocks:** "I'll carry the family's pain for them." (Keeps your field heavy.)

Prompt:

- "What promise did I make to myself or life to feel safe, loved, or accepted?"

Step 2 – Honor Why You Made It

Every promise started as protection. Instead of judging, thank it.

- *"I see that I made this promise to protect myself from rejection."*
- *"I made this vow to belong in my family system."*

This acknowledgment reduces shame and allows you to release it with compassion.

Step 3 – Ask: Is It Still True?

Check the promise against your current reality.

- "Does keeping this promise help me expand—or hold me back?"
- "If I keep living by this vow, what will it cost me?"
- "What would be possible if I released it?"

Step 4 – Rewrite the Promise

Create a new, aligned commitment. Examples:

- Old: *"I'll never need anyone."*
  → New: *"I allow myself to receive support while staying strong."*
- Old: *"I must always sacrifice for others."*
  → New: *"I give with love, but not at the cost of my well-being."*
- Old: *"Money always leaves."*
  → New: *"I create, keep, and grow wealth in alignment with my values."*

Step 5 – Ritualize the Release

Your subconscious responds to symbols. Use one of these:

- **Fire:** Write the old promise on paper, burn it safely, and say, *"This vow is complete."*
- **Water:** Speak it aloud into water, then pour it out (bath, river, sink) as a release.
- **Earth:** Bury the note/object that represents the promise, saying, *"I return this to the earth."*

- **Air:** Breathe deeply, exhale while saying the old promise, inhale while saying the new one.

Step 6 – Anchor the New

Put the new promise into practice immediately. Small steps matter.

- If your new promise is about receiving support → ask for help today.
- If your new promise is about abundance → save or invest a small amount.
- If your new promise is about love → allow yourself to accept kindness without deflecting.

You don't "break" promises so much as **update them**. What once kept you safe may now keep you small. By honoring the old, releasing it with compassion, and anchoring the new, you clear blocks across every level—emotional, mental, energetic, physical, inherited, and relational.

To Others *(with Integrity)*

Step 1 – Identify the Promise

Notice the commitment you made that now feels heavy or misaligned. Examples:

- **Inherited:** Carrying on a family role or tradition that limits you.
- **Emotional:** Always being the "strong one" for a friend.
- **Mental:** Promising always to follow someone else's way of doing things.
- **Physical:** Overcommitting to tasks, projects, or caregiving beyond your capacity.

- **Conflict:** Promising "I'll never disagree" to keep peace in a relationship.
- **Energetic:** Agreeing to stay tied into a draining relationship.

Reflection Prompt:

- "What promise did I make to someone else that no longer fits who I am or what I can sustain?"

Step 2 – Acknowledge Why You Said Yes

You probably made the promise out of love, duty, fear of loss, or wanting acceptance. Instead of guilt, acknowledge the positive intent.

- *"I promised this because I cared about them and wanted to help."*
- *"I agreed because I thought it was the only way to belong."*

Step 3 – Get Clear on the Cost

Ask:

- "What does keeping this promise cost me (time, health, alignment, relationships)?"
- "What will it cost the other person if I keep living in resentment?"

This reframes breaking the promise as an act of honesty and long-term care.

Step 4 – Decide the New Boundary or Agreement

What can you offer instead?

- Old: *"I'll always drop everything for you."*
  → New: *"I love you, but I can't be on call 24/7. Here's what I can do."*
- Old: *"I'll stay in this business partnership forever."*
  → New: *"This chapter feels complete. I'd like to support you in transitioning smoothly."*
- Old: *"I'll carry this family tradition no matter what."*
  → New: *"I honor our history, but I need to create my own path."*

Step 5 – Communicate with Compassion

When possible, have a direct conversation. Use "I" statements and compassion.

- *"I want to be honest. When I made this promise, it felt right. But now I realize I can't keep it without harming myself."*
- *"This doesn't mean I don't care about you. It means I want to show up in a way that's sustainable and true."*
- *"Here's what I can offer instead…"*

Step 6 – Release Guilt, Hold Integrity

Breaking a promise doesn't mean breaking trust—**hiding and resenting does that.** By being honest and compassionate, you model alignment. Sometimes others will resist, but over time, clear and honest boundaries create stronger relationships.

Ritual for Closure:

If direct conversation isn't possible (e.g., person is no longer alive, safe, or in contact):

- Write them a letter you don't send.
- Say the words aloud in meditation: *"I release myself from this promise. I send you love and wish you freedom as well."*
- Imagine cutting or dissolving cords between you, filling the space with light.

Breaking a promise to others doesn't mean abandoning love or loyalty—it means updating the agreement so that both people can grow in truth, rather than stay stuck in resentment or illusion.

How to Know When a Block Has Cleared

Clearing blocks is only part of the journey. The deeper work lies in **integration**—anchoring the shift so it lasts. This is where lightness, clarity, and freedom become part of who you are, not just fleeting relief. Integration teaches your body, mind, and energy field to remember what empowerment feels like, so you can return to it again and again.

Integration is never about force. It is about **presence, humility, and gratitude**—meeting yourself in a new way and letting that become your foundation.

SIGNS A BLOCK HAS CLEARED

Inherited / Collective Blocks

- Old family or cultural "rules" no longer dictate your choices.
- You feel free to create your own patterns instead of repeating ancestral ones.
- Guilt about "surpassing" others fades, replaced by acceptance and pride.

Emotional Blocks

- A sense of release replaces the weight of disappointment, resentment, jealousy, or guilt.
- You no longer replay the story in your head.
- Gratitude, peace, or curiosity naturally take the place of old emotional tension.

Mental Blocks

- Thoughts feel spacious instead of looping or rigid.
- Self-doubt softens, replaced by a quiet trust in your capacity.
- You can hold new perspectives without the old narrative pulling you back.

Physical Blocks

- Chronic tightness, fatigue, or tension begins to ease.
- Movement feels freer, posture more open, and sleep more restful.
- You notice you have more energy to act on your goals.

Conflict Blocks

- Relationships feel less tangled or draining.
- You can hold your vision without collapsing when others disagree.
- Boundaries feel clearer, and you no longer carry responsibility that isn't yours.

Energetic Blocks

- Your body feels lighter, as if static has lifted.
- Breathing deepens naturally, shoulders soften, and flow returns.
- You sense clarity in your aura or energy field, with less heaviness or "stickiness."

ANCHORING CONFIDENCE THROUGH REFLECTION RITUALS

- **Daily:** Write down one action, thought, or choice that showed you trusted yourself. Even the smallest wins count.
- **Weekly:** Reflect on when your energy, body, or relationships felt clear—what supported that state?
- **Manifestation-Specific:** After a shift or achievement, pause to integrate. Journal, light a candle, walk in nature, or speak gratitude aloud to mark the moment.

Practices for Staying in Humility and Gratitude

- Morning mantra: *"Thank you for another chance to show up in truth."*
- Evening ritual: Recall 3 moments you're grateful for, no matter how small.
- Notice when ego tries to overtake confidence—redirect to service, curiosity, and openness.

Building "Confidence Memory"

Confidence strengthens when it is embodied, not just thought. Each time you clear a block, pause to notice:

- Shoulders relaxed yet lifted.
- Breathing steady and full.
- Heart open, voice steady.
- Mind calm, body grounded, energy flowing.

By bringing awareness to these sensations, you create a "memory" your system can return to whenever fear or doubt arises.

Journaling Prompts

- "The moment I knew a block had cleared was when I felt…"
- "Confidence in my body feels like…"
- "The ritual that best anchors my empowerment is…"
- "What part of me is freer now that this block is gone?"

Why This Works

Confidence doesn't come from perfection or control—it comes from **remembering who you are when you are free of blocks.** Integration ensures that clarity isn't temporary but woven into your being. Through reflection, gratitude, and embodied awareness, you train your system to return to confidence naturally, no matter what new challenges arise.

Appendix

The DREAM Method

D – Drift (Unconscious Thought: the spark, the first glimpse)
Every manifestation begins as a passing drift of thought. These "drift-thoughts" float through the mind almost unnoticed — subtle, fleeting, yet full of potential. Though you may not pay attention, Spirit hears them all.

R – Recognize (bringing unconscious into consciousness)
When you choose to notice and hold a thought, you bring it into focus. Recognition turns random sparks into intentional seeds. This is where you clarify and commit.

E – Execute (aligned action, practical and decisive)
Dreams need energy. Taking small, aligned steps — writing it down, speaking it, preparing for it — tells Spirit and your subconscious: *"I am serious."* Execution is the bridge from mind to matter.

A – Achieve (Manifest: live it)
The desire materializes. You step into the experience of what you once only imagined. This is the moment where thought becomes reality — the fruit of alignment, action, and Spirit's partnership.

M – Master (Evolve: reflect, refine, and repeat)
Every manifestation brings wisdom. Mastery means reflecting on what worked, what didn't, and how it shaped you. With

mastery, you evolve — ready to dream again, even bigger, even clearer.

Bibliography

Manifestation & Personal Development

- Robbins, Tony. *Awaken the Giant Within.* New York: Free Press, 1991.
- Dyer, Wayne. *Manifest Your Destiny.* New York: HarperCollins, 1997.
- Hay, Louise. *You Can Heal Your Life.* Carlsbad: Hay House, 1984.
- Tolle, Eckhart. *The Power of Now.* Novato: New World Library, 1999.
- Hicks, Esther and Jerry. *Ask and It Is Given.* Carlsbad: Hay House, 2004.

Psychology, Ego, & Self-Sabotage

- Brown, Brené. *The Gifts of Imperfection.* Center City: Hazelden, 2010.
- Kegan, Robert, and Lahey, Lisa. *Immunity to Change.* Boston: Harvard Business Press, 2009.
- Young, Jeffrey E., Klosko, Janet S., and Weishaar, Marjorie E. *Schema Therapy: A Practitioner's Guide.* New York: Guilford Press, 2003.
- Baumeister, Roy F. *The Self in Social Psychology.* Philadelphia: Psychology Press, 1999.

Energy Healing & Somatic Practices

- Brennan, Barbara Ann. *Hands of Light.* New York: Bantam, 1987.
- Levine, Peter A. *Waking the Tiger: Healing Trauma.* Berkeley: North Atlantic Books, 1997.

- Siegel, Daniel J. *The Mindful Brain.* New York: W.W. Norton, 2007.
- Myss, Caroline. *Anatomy of the Spirit.* New York: Three Rivers Press, 1996.
- Oschman, James L. *Energy Medicine: The Scientific Basis.* London: Churchill Livingstone, 2000.

Meditation, Breathwork, & Spiritual Practices

- Nestor, James. *Breath: The New Science of a Lost Art.* New York: Riverhead Books, 2020.
- Kabat-Zinn, Jon. *Wherever You Go, There You Are.* New York: Hyperion, 1994.
- Chopra, Deepak. *Quantum Healing.* New York: Bantam, 1989.
- Hanh, Thich Nhat. *The Miracle of Mindfulness.* Boston: Beacon Press, 1975.

Message From The Author

When I wrote *Manifestation – The DREAM Method in 5 Steps*, I wanted to help you understand how to create what you desire. But as every true creator learns, the deeper work begins not in the manifesting—but in the mastering.

This book is about what happens *after* the wish comes true. It's about the quiet, powerful space where you realize that keeping your success, peace, or purpose requires a new level of self-trust. Here, manifestation matures into confidence, and confidence becomes a living expression of mastery.

True mastery doesn't mean you no longer face doubt—it means you've learned to meet it with presence and grace. It's the moment when your faith no longer wavers with circumstance, when gratitude becomes your default setting, and when you trust yourself enough to stay aligned even when the outcome isn't yet visible.

Confidence is not arrogance—it is the gentle knowing that you are guided, capable, and supported. It is the bridge between the vision and the lived experience, between dreaming and doing, between creating and keeping.

My hope is that these practices help you anchor what you've manifested into the fabric of your daily life. That you move through the world with steady light, clear purpose, and open heart. That you come to know confidence not as something to chase—but as something that already lives within you, waiting to be remembered.

With faith in your mastery and belief in your light,
Dr. Constance Santego

Live the DREAM: Drift, Recognize, Execute, Achieve, Master.

About the Author

Dr. Constance Santego, Ph.D., DNM, is a bestselling author, educator, and holistic practitioner with over two decades of experience in natural medicine, energy healing, and transformational teaching. Renowned for blending ancient wisdom with modern understanding, she has guided thousands of students worldwide through her courses, books, and workshops on manifestation, Reiki, bioenergetics, and mind-body healing.

As the author of more than forty books spanning both fiction and nonfiction, Dr. Santego explores the bridge between science and spirit—revealing how awareness, frequency, and energy shape the human experience. Her work reflects her belief that true healing and manifestation begin with self-mastery: when the mind, body, and spirit unite in confidence, transformation becomes sustainable.

Her signature **DREAM Method** (Drift, Recognize, Execute, Achieve, Master) was developed to make manifestation practical, repeatable, and deeply personal. In this second volume, she expands that vision—teaching how to move beyond creation into embodiment, where success and confidence become lived realities.

When she is not teaching or writing, Dr. Santego continues her mission to empower others by mentoring entrepreneurs, creating transformative courses, and inspiring communities through her YouTube channel and speaking engagements. She lives in beautiful British Columbia, where she enjoys nature, family, and the everyday magic of living what she teaches.

ALSO AVAILABLE

For additional information on

Constance Santego's

wide range of Motivational Products, Coaching Sessions,
Spiritual Retreats,
Live Events and Educational Programs

Go to

www.ConstanceSantego.ca

Follow on Instagram - Constance_Santego and
Facebook - constancesantegoo

Subscribe and receive Free Information and Meditations
on her
YouTube Channel - Constance Santego

If you've studied with me before, you may recognize echoes of what I taught in my *Fairy Tales, Dreams, and Reality* course and *The Art of Manifestation*. This book is the evolution of those teachings — updated, expanded, and reshaped into a method that is both practical and profound. The DREAM Method is the next step in a journey we have been on together, designed to guide you more clearly than ever before.

Manifestation – The DREAM Method in 5 Steps
Softcover: Available at **Barnes &
Noble, Indigo/Chapters, and Amazon**
Soft Cover ISBN: 978-1-990062-85-8

Fairytales, Dreams, and Reality: *Where are you on your path?* **Softcover:** Available at **Barnes & Noble, Indigo/Chapters, and Amazon**
Soft Cover ISBN: 978-1-990062-15-5

www.ingramcontent.com/pod-product-compliance
Lightning Source LLC
Chambersburg PA
CBHW071735120626
46550CB00002B/527